Big Ideas of Early Mathematics

What Teachers of Young Children Need to Know

The Early Math Collaborative

Erikson Institute

Boston   Columbus   Indianapolis   New York   San Francisco   Upper Saddle River
Amsterdam   Cape Town   Dubai   London   Madrid   Milan   Munich   Paris   Montréal   Toronto
Delhi   Mexico City   São Paulo   Sydney   Hong Kong   Seoul   Singapore   Taipei   Tokyo

Vice President and Editorial Director:
 Jeffery W. Johnston
Senior Acquisitions Editor: Julie Peters
Editorial Assistant: Andrea Hall
Vice President and Director of Marketing:
 Margaret Waples
Senior Marketing Manager: Christine Gatchell
Senior Managing Editor: Pamela D. Bennett
Production Project Manager: Carrie Mollette
Procurement Specialist: Michelle Klein

Senior Art Director: Laura Gardner
Cover Art: Steven E. Gross
Media Project Manager: Noelle Chun
Full-Service Project Management:
 Mary Tindle, S4Carlisle Publishing Services
Composition: S4Carlisle Publishing Services
Printer/Binder: Courier/Westford
Cover Printer: Courier/Westford
Text Font: Guardi LT Std 9.75/13

Credits and acknowledgments for material borrowed from other sources and reproduced, with permission, in this textbook appear on the appropriate page within the text.

Every effort has been made to provide accurate and current Internet information in this book. However, the Internet and information posted on it are constantly changing, so it is inevitable that some of the Internet addresses listed in this textbook will change.

Photo Credits: Steven E. Gross, Front cover, pp. 2, 12, 28, 46, 64, 82, 98, 112, 130, 146, 168; Michael Paulucci, pp. 59, 126, Back cover.

Library of Congress Cataloging-in-Publication Data
Brownell, Jeanine O'Nan.
 Big ideas of early mathematics: what teachers of young children need to know / Jeanine O'Nan Brownell (M.S.), Jie-Qi Chen (Ph.D.), Lisa Ginet (Ed.D.); The Early Math Collaborative Erikson Institute.—First edition.
 pages cm
 Includes bibliographical references and index.
 ISBN 978-0-13-294697-1
1. Mathematics—Study and teaching (Early childhood) I. Chen, Jie-Qi. II. Ginet, Lisa.
III. Erikson Institute. Early Math Collaborative. IV. Title.
 QA135.6.B766 2014
 372.7'044—dc23
                                                                        2013005299

10 9 8 7 6 5 4

ISBN 10:   0-13-294697-1
ISBN 13: 978-0-13-294697-1

Brief Contents

Contents

About the Authors

The author of this book is not an individual but a group of devoted early childhood specialists who are part of The Early Math Collaborative at Erikson Institute.

Brownell, Jeanine O'Nan, M.S., has extensive curriculum writing experience. She worked at the Center for Elementary Mathematics and Science Education at the University of Chicago. While there, she revised the first-grade component of the *Everyday Mathematics,* Third Edition curriculum and authored *Pre-Kindergarten Everyday Mathematics.* Jeanine has many years of experience as a classroom teacher of first, second, and third grades. She also has mentored new teachers and worked as an instructional coach.

Chen, Jie-Qi, Ph.D., is the Principal Investigator of the Collaborative and Professor of Child Development at Erikson Institute. She has taught preschool, elementary, and middle schools in China and preschool and kindergarten in the United States. She has contributed to teacher professional development efforts for more than 20 years. Jie-Qi has published six books and numerous articles. She is the 2009 recipient of the Outstanding Teacher Educator's Award from the National Association of Early Childhood Teacher Educators, a Fulbright Senior Specialist in Education, and a consultant to UNICEF and the Ministry of Education in China.

Ginet, Lisa, Ed.D., has spent more than two decades as a professional educator in various positions (classroom teacher, child care provider, parent educator, home visitor, teacher trainer, adjunct faculty) in diverse settings (child care centers, elementary and middle schools, family resource agency, family child care home, community college, private university). In all her roles, Lisa has worked to engage children in active and meaningful learning, to support families as their children's first and closest teachers, and to involve educators in reflective and practical dialogue to help improve their teaching.

Hynes-Berry, Mary, Ph.D., is on the faculty at Erikson Institute. She has been involved in preservice and in-service work with teachers and with young children for over 30 years, with an emphasis on early literacy, mathematics, and science. Her background includes many years of using oral storytelling as the basis of curriculum in schools. Mary credits her work as the project director of Encyclopedia Britannica's Early Math project for deepening her understanding of foundational mathematics. She is the author of two books and several articles.

Itzkowich, Rebeca, M.A., is a senior instructor in the teacher education and bilingual/ESL certification programs at Erikson Institute. She has taught preschool and elementary school in Mexico, Spain, and the United States. For the past 10 years, Rebeca has provided professional development to teachers in the areas of culturally and linguistically responsive teaching. As a member of The Early Math Collaborative at Erikson, she has worked to help teachers discover a love for foundational mathematics and collaborated with instructional math coaches to inspire teachers to become more reflective about their mathematics teaching.

Johnson, Donna, M.S., taught elementary math in a private school setting for 8 years. For 7 years, she served as co-director of an academic enrichment program serving homeschool families, and provided instruction in math and science for 3rd–8th grade. For the past twelve years, Donna has conducted parent workshops and provided professional development and coaching to teachers and child care providers in literacy and math. As a coach and coach supervisor, Donna provides support to coaches and teachers in The Early Math Collaborative, helping them to deepen their understanding of foundational math and be more reflective in their practice.

McCray, Jennifer, Ph.D., is the Director of The Early Math Collaborative and an Assistant Research Scientist at Erikson Institute. She is a former preschool teacher, with over 10 years experience in teacher training. Her dissertation, which focused on preschool teachers' knowledge of early mathematics, won two national awards—one from Division K (Teaching and Teacher Education) of the American Educational Research Association, and another from the National Association of Early Childhood Teacher Educators.

Foreword

Aside from counting, number recognition, and naming two-dimensional shapes, math is often given short shrift during the early school years. This is despite recent findings from neuroscience that show the roots of later mathematical competence are established long before middle school, confirming the importance of the link between early experience and subsequent achievement. Because of this link, we must be sure that children's experience is sufficient to activate their potential and prepare them for the challenges of the 21st century.

Even without organized curricula and instruction, young children develop an informal knowledge of math concepts through their interactions with people and things. Children have many opportunities to consider and compare numbers of objects, to gain knowledge of spatial relationships, and to use these budding understandings to solve simple problems (bringing two cookies to the table, one for me, and one for a friend). The process of constructing math knowledge is natural and well-established by the time children are 3 years old.

Although all children have enough experience touching and observing objects to learn that three crayons are more than two crayons, it takes an adult or older child to help them learn the written numerals, much less algebra and calculus. Children's own actions and observations are not enough; they need specific instruction to deepen and extend their knowledge and skills. Two kinds of experience are necessary: one type is guided by the child and arises from his own actions; the other occurs as teachers (parents, older children) give information that challenges her current understanding. Mathematical knowledge is built on both kinds of experience.

Big Ideas of Early Mathematics: What Teachers of Young Children Need to Know by The Early Math Collaborative pays attention to both kinds of experiences: those that children can engage in on their own, interacting with materials (ideas with a nudge from a thoughtful teacher); and those that are planned and facilitated by the teacher. This text also provides an incredibly rich set of activities for both teachers and parents, and more importantly, points out why these are important. Given the meager background in mathematical knowledge of many Americans and some early childhood teachers this text is welcome. It will go a long way toward filling the gaps in teacher knowledge about mathematics and its teaching for young children.

Barbara T. Bowman
Erikson Institute

Preface

Once upon a time, Dr. Jie-Qi Chen conducted a survey of preschool teachers in the Chicago Public Schools. She found that while they felt mathematical learning was important for their young charges, they also felt ill-prepared to guide it. Many preschool teachers reported that they did not enjoy math themselves and were uncertain what math content they needed to teach.

Lucky for us, Jie-Qi is a Professor at Erikson Institute, a graduate school in child development in Chicago. Erikson specializes in the training of leaders in many fields that have anything to do with children between the ages of 0 and 8 and their families, so there were plenty of people there who had experience in and thought about early childhood teaching.

Jie-Qi first turned to her doctoral student, Jennifer McCray, who was completing a dissertation on what preschool teachers know about early math; and together they gathered a group of experienced teacher educators, including Mary Hynes-Berry, Rebeca Itzkowich, and Jeanine O'Nan Brownell. With generous funding from the Robert R. McCormick Foundation and CME Group Foundation, Erikson's Early Mathematics Education Project was launched. From its inception, the goal of the project has been to help teachers develop the mathematics competencies they need to provide quality mathematics education to children during the critical years of early schooling.

Based on their conviction that early childhood teachers needed to understand early math content better, they began to study it themselves. They read many books and articles about early math and cognitive development, struggling to explain the mathematics to one another, and worked to create simple statements about important math concepts. Along the way, they were joined by seasoned instructors Lisa Ginet and Donna Johnson; and eventually, this team developed the Big Ideas of Early Mathematics, on which this book is based.

This team also created and implemented extensive teacher training along the way, working with both pre-K and kindergarten teachers from schools all over the city of Chicago and beyond. To make their training effective, they borrowed the idea of the "whole child" to develop the "Whole Teacher Approach" to professional development. The idea was that, just as teachers of young children had to think about child development in an integrated way, trainers of teachers had to think about teacher development as an interaction among teachers' knowledge for teaching, their attitudes about teaching, and their teaching practices. Because of this, their training focused explicitly on the Big Ideas (knowledge), had an emphasis on fun and confidence building (attitudes), and included research lessons that teachers tried out with children between training sessions and classroom-based individual coaching (practice). And guess what: it worked!

They studied the effects of the training, and found that children in the classrooms of teachers in their program learned more mathematics during a single school year—almost three months more on average—than children in other classrooms. They were so excited by this that they applied for and won a large federal grant that allowed them to expand their training to include first-, second-, and third-grade teachers.

We don't know how this story ends yet, because the Erikson Early Math Project continues to grow. Now encompassing several projects, and collaborating with teachers, teacher educators, and researchers nationwide, we are known as The Early Math Collaborative. Nevertheless, we are still developing and providing training, trying to make sure that children everywhere get the excellent and fun foundation in early mathematics that they deserve. We do know, however, that the Big Ideas of Early Mathematics that apply especially well to preschool and kindergarten are ready to be shared with more people, and that is the purpose of this book.

We at The Early Math Collaborative hope that more people than just early childhood teachers will read this text. Generally, teachers of older children, and most adults do not have a solid understanding of the Big Ideas of Early Mathematics. Those first mental leaps we humans make as we explore quantities, shapes, and sizes are enormous in their scope, highly abstract, and generally complex. Understanding this well can make it easier to teach math with children of all ages, creating profound appreciation for the flexibility and elegance of human thought, even among our youngest children.

For all of our dear readers, we hope you enjoy this text. It is our sincere belief that this book will inspire you to see mathematics in your daily life and to talk about it with confidence and passion!

—The Early Math Collaborative
earlymath.erikson.edu

Acknowledgments

The work described here was supported by grants from the Robert R. McCormick Foundation, CME Group Foundation, Motorola Solutions Foundation, the Office of Early Childhood Education in the Chicago Public Schools, Exelon Foundation, and The Robert and Isabelle Bass Foundation, Inc. We are grateful to the generous funders who make The Early Math Collaborative's work possible.

Two Early Math Collaborative staff members in particular deserve mention: Cody Meirick and Suzanne Budak use their considerable talents daily to enhance the work of the entire team. Margaret Adams and Colleen Sims were instrumental in reading early drafts of this book.

Our sincere thanks also go to hundreds of teachers who have participated in the teacher professional development program of The Early Math Collaborative. They tested our Big Ideas in the classroom, provided valuable feedback, and informed us of the usefulness of these Big Ideas in helping them understand foundational mathematics. It is their encouraging voice and improved practice that is the driving force behind this text.

We would also like to thank the reviewers of the drafts of this book for their constructive comments: Myrna Scott Amos, Duval County Public Schools; Connie Casha, Tennessee Department of Education; Karen Crider, Middle Georgia RESA; Pam Hibbs, Oklahoma City Public Schools; and Pamela L. Shue, University of North Carolina at Charlotte.

Introduction

Why Focus on Big Ideas?

Math Snapshot

Tracy loves coming up with great literacy activities in her preschool classroom. She carefully picks out her daily read-aloud and knows the advantages of revisiting a wonderful story. She sees the value in doing story dictation and dramatization as a natural and playful way to help children develop phonemic awareness and a sense of narrative.

As confident as Tracy is about her ability to address literacy, she worries about what happens in her classroom when it comes to math. She has a daily calendar routine and uses some recorded counting songs at least every other day. Still, she is frustrated that she's not really sure what her 4-year-olds and 5-year-olds *ought* to understand about mathematics—much less how to assess and develop their understanding. Underlying everything else is a nagging feeling that she doesn't really like math and never has—she hopes she is not communicating this to the children.

Do you share some of Tracy's concerns about math in your own classroom? If so, you are by no means alone. There is strong evidence that American early childhood professionals spend significantly more time on literacy than on mathematics. Most also feel more confident they can help produce lifelong readers than prepare children to enjoy math. Recent research, however, has shown that early math competence is one of the best predictors of school success *across the curriculum*. Moreover, as the world continues to move into an age where many jobs that require a strong understanding of mathematics are at the heart of technological advancement, it may be especially important that we get better at preparing young children to excel mathematically.

The fact that you are reading this book suggests that you, like Tracy, are one of the many dedicated early childhood professionals who is eager to learn how you can do better when it comes to math. As teacher educators with years of experience, at the Early Math Collaborative, we are confident that early childhood teachers like you can be terrific math advocates for young children—you simply need better information about what early math *is*. This book is meant to help you fill that void, since we believe that *you have to understand what you are teaching to teach for understanding.*

This conviction is based on our experiences working with teachers like you at Erikson Institute. It has been our privilege to provide training in foundational mathematics to more than 400 Chicago Public School preschool, kindergarten, and Head Start teachers. These teachers have been our partners in exploring the Big Ideas that underlie all mathematical procedures; they worked with us to help us understand how to make these basic ideas clear to young children. We found that teachers in our program were able to make significant improvements in children's math learning—in fact, children who were behind at the beginning of the school year began to catch up to their peers.

More importantly, we heard again and again how useful it was to teachers to better understand early math content. Many teachers who "didn't like math" became inspired math teachers, seeing how mathematical situations are in children's literature and everyday routines, and communicating their own excitement to children on a daily basis.

We are confident that a focus on the Big Ideas is a key element of their success. This book is meant to help you deepen your own understanding, and as a result, change your perspective on mathematics. We also hope that as you explore the Big Ideas, your confidence will grow so that you, like the teachers with whom we have worked, will find that teaching math is actually fun!

What Are Big Ideas?

Math Snapshot

After a day of training with the Early Math Collaborative, Tracy stopped the instructor to share her excitement about an insight she had that day. "Up to now," Tracy said, "I hadn't ever thought there were any *ideas* involved in counting—I just considered it a skill. The children either could do it or they needed more practice. But, all that changed when you showed the Big Ideas Chart and we talked about children's cardinal understanding: the idea of 'three-ness.' I can't wait to get back to class and find out which of my students really understands just how many three is!"

Tracy's realization that children must not only be able to say the counting words in order, but that they also need to understand that three is an amount—more than two, less than four—is just the kind of thinking we hope the Big Ideas will inspire. In order to be a "Big Idea," a concept must meet the three criteria identified by Clements and Sarama (2009). A Big Idea is:

- *Mathematically central and coherent.* Big Ideas convey core mathematics concepts and skills that can serve as organizing structures for teaching and learning during early childhood years.

- *Consistent with children's thinking.* Big Ideas build on young children's informal or everyday mathematical knowledge and promote the scientific understanding of basic mathematical concepts and the development of logical mathematical thinking.

- *Generative of future learning.* Big Ideas provide foundations for further mathematics learning and facilitate long-lasting mathematical understanding.

We have taken the most current research from the fields of cognitive science and mathematics education to create a set of **26 Big Ideas:** key mathematical concepts that lay the foundation for lifelong mathematical learning and thinking. While these concepts can be explored at an early age, they are powerful enough that children can and should engage with them for years to come. Examples of Big Ideas are presented in chart form in Table i.1.

We have also paid close attention to practical concerns about alignment with standards and ease of implementation. For these reasons, our Big Ideas are:

- *Comprehensive.* The Big Ideas are closely aligned with the content of the Common Core State Standards (2010) and reflect the emphasis defined by the National Council of Teachers of Mathematics' (NCTM) Curriculum Focal

TABLE i.1   Sample Big Ideas Chart

Topic	Big Ideas	Examples
Uses of Number = 5 5ᵗʰ	• Numbers are used many ways, including: • to indicate amount. (cardinal) • to specify position in a sequence. (ordinal) • to provide names for members of a set. (nominal) • to act as shared reference points. (referential)	• Tommy has five books. (cardinal) • Ava is fifth in line today. (ordinal) • Numbers on basketball jerseys, home addresses, telephone numbers (nominal) • "Let's meet at 5 p.m. on December 5." (referential)
Counting "1, 2, 3, 4, 5 . . . 5!"	• Counting can be used to find out *how many* in a collection. • Counting has rules that apply to any collection. • Counting words have to be said in the same order every time. • Each object in a set must be counted once and only once. • It does not matter in what order the objects within a set are counted. • The last number word produced is the amount of the entire set.	• "1, 2, 3, 4, 5, you have five stars!" • "One, four, two" doesn't give a correct answer. • Children need strategies for keeping track, like touch-pointing or moving to another pile. • Mixing up objects and counting again is a good exercise; the third object counted is not the only one that can "be" three. • Being able to count is not the same as being able to answer "how many?"

Points (NCTM, 2006). You can be confident that these Big Ideas provide a complete framework for planning your early math teaching.

- *Thoughtful about content.* We have clustered our 26 Big Ideas into nine topic areas, with a chapter devoted to each one. If you examine the table at the end of this chapter, you will see that there are more chapters here about number and operations than anything else. This is a conscious choice and reflects our sense of what an early childhood classroom ought to emphasize.

- *Developmentally organized.* Within each chapter topic, we present the Big Ideas in an order that makes clear how later ideas can be built upon and refer back to those presented earlier. While we do not claim that math concepts develop among all children in exactly the sequence presented here, the list is developmentally based. We believe this sequence will be helpful to your own understanding of the ideas and how they show up in the learning of children.

- *Flexible.* The Big Ideas are not meant to add a new set of activities to your workload. Instead, we hope they complement your current math teaching, enriching your understanding and allowing a more nuanced and powerful implementation of curriculum. Understanding this set of ideas should be as helpful to you during free play in the block corner as it is during circle time when you are counting how many children are present today.

In short, the Big Ideas map the key math concepts young children should be wrestling with between the ages of 3 and 6. The point is not to have the children recite them, but for you to explore them and deepen your own mathematical understanding. When you understand the Big Ideas well yourself, you can notice and take advantage of the ways that math is all around us in early childhood classrooms. This knowledge will also help you recognize the kinds of structured activities that do the best job of making these ideas real for young children, which means you will be able to make them fun without losing the important concepts under the "glitter and glue." And, once you know how these ideas develop in the thinking of young children, you will be able to more easily determine what children in your class do and do not understand and to know what types of math concepts and experiences they ought to be exposed to next.

 # Building Your Approach to Early Math

Because the focus of this text is on deepening understanding of the Big Ideas, you will see some—but not many—activity ideas; good curricula will provide plenty more of those. However, in our discussion of the Big Ideas and what classrooms that use them look like, we will return again and again to a few key **strategic teaching practices**.

These **practices** are pedagogical methods we use repeatedly; in fact, they are so deeply imbedded in our beliefs about the best ways to help children understand math that they can be called "habits of mind." At the same time, these practices should be used **strategically**; that is, when we decide which practice to focus on in a particular case, we factor in what we know about the general developmental trajectory of the Big Ideas as well as the needs and interests of young children. It's not always possible or appropriate to use all the practices at once, so we discuss them throughout the text where they make the most sense to us. Below, we briefly outline these five strategic teaching practices.

1. *Mathematize the world around us.* In recent years, the term **mathematize** has emerged to express the importance of helping children engage with the mathematics that is all around us. Just as a photographer can use different lenses to capture the world in different ways, we hope that early childhood teachers will begin to look at the world through a "math lens." Teachers who do so are always working to "see" the math around them and to be alert to the way that math and mathematical problem situations are built into the very fabric of their lives. Mathematizing means that as adults, we offer feedback that helps children see the math underlying these situations and that we are purposeful in inviting the children to take an active role in problem solving. It also suggests the usefulness of looking to meaningful situations to help children think about math, rather than constructing "false" or arbitrary activities that have no connection to their lives.

2. *Make mathematics more than the manipulatives.* Parents and early childhood professionals know instinctively that young children need concrete learning experiences. The younger they are, the more they need to move themselves or objects around so that they explore and make sense of their environment. Most preschool classrooms are well stocked with objects like unit blocks and counters, but simply having them in the classroom does not guarantee learning. Children must be helped to use them for mathematical purposes. Moreover, math experiences must be more than just "hands on," because math, even from the start, is abstract. Mathematics can and should be represented in multiple ways, as children must make connections between concrete experiences, symbols, pictures, and language.

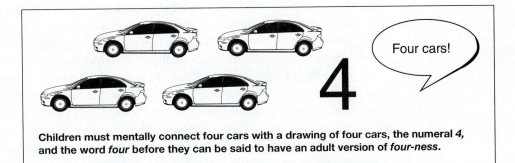

Children must mentally connect four cars with a drawing of four cars, the numeral *4*, and the word *four* before they can be said to have an adult version of *four-ness*.

While concrete representations of ideas are the most basic, written symbols are the most abstract and advanced. Pictures of things can bridge this divide since they are just one step removed from the real thing. For example, a drawing of four cars has more in common with a real group of four cars than the numeral "4" has. Adding four dots next to the numeral provides an additional clue to help children make the abstraction. Because connections between concrete, pictorial, and symbolic representations are neither automatic nor static, we need to continually plan intentional activities that allow children to move back and forth between concrete, pictorial, and symbolic versions of ideas. Doing so provides them with many different ways to "get" the idea, while building fluidity into their mathematical thinking and preparing them for more complex mathematics to come.

3. *Recognize receptive understanding.* Think about how a toddler who can manage to speak only four or five words clearly understands many, many more. This phenomenon holds true for learning a new language at any age, as well as learning other skills, such as reading musical notes or programming computers. In terms of mathematical understanding, it's often true that a child who can compare two bowls and select the one that has four tiles in it may not be able to count out a set of four tiles when presented with an entire bowlful. While she can *find* the bowl with four tiles (receptive understanding), she cannot yet *create* it (productive understanding).

As we will see again and again, the importance of recognizing receptive understanding takes on special force when teachers work with young children whose language skills are just developing. Teachers of the very young need to be especially alert to *nonverbal indications of what a child is thinking*, including gestures and actions. All children's language development benefits greatly from positive feedback that acknowledges, reinforces, or offers clarification of what the child is attempting to communicate.

Mathematical language poses special challenges for young children because it often focuses on abstractions. *Big*, *little*, and even *five* all describe attributes instead of things. That is, they focus on a quality shared by more than one object, rather than an object itself—it is much harder to get the idea of "round" than the idea of "chair." Then, there are all the math words that are about comparisons, like *heavier*, *shorter*, *less*, and *more*. Again, there is not an object here—it is a *relationship between* objects that is being described. Developmentally, the more abstract an idea, the more time it takes for children to make good sense of the word that signifies it in any language.

Many children arrive in early childhood classrooms with a home language other than English. These English Language Learners, especially those who are at the early stages of English language acquisition, may have a good conceptual grasp of a Big Idea but may not be able to talk about it in English. Or, they may be in need of specialized mathematical language to express their ideas; their challenge is a linguistic one. For this reason, children whose dominant language is not English should be encouraged to use their home language to talk about mathematical ideas. That will mean creating group-ings where math investigations and discussions are occurring in the children's home language. Teachers can then use either bilingual adults or children who are becoming more fluent in English to share what was said in the small group discussion. In all cases, teachers who make a conscious effort to look for and recognize evidence of receptive understanding of mathematical ideas have an advantage in working with English Language Learners and all young children.

4. *Get mathematics into children's eyes, ears, hands, and feet.* A day in the life of a pre-schooler is filled with many opportunities for singing, jumping, dancing, and storytelling. While these activities are no doubt engaging for the children, they also offer opportunities for multimodal learning. In essence, multimodal learning refers to a learning situation that engages multiple sensory and ac-tion systems of the learner. Auditory inputs might include an activity like singing a counting song to help children learn the number word sequence, while kinesthetic activities might include marching to a drumbeat to get a feel for one-to-one correspondence. Brain research confirms that, at all stages of development, the more modes the learner accesses, the deeper the learning.

Anyone who works or lives with young children knows that nothing is more delightful than returning to favorite routines and stories again and again and again—and yet again. If the initial experience was positive, each revisit-ing has a "value-added" effect. But if there are no new twists and no sense of positive spirit and playfulness, no invitation to celebrate how you understand a little more because you've done this before—well, then, drill will kill! There is a place for memorization in math, since, for example, everyone has to even-tually memorize the number words and be able to say them in the right order. But, when the words are connected to real and interesting things, like how many children are here today or how many days until our class party, they become so much more meaningful and much easier to learn.

When new ideas are presented in many different ways, learners' brains form more connections between those new ideas and other things that they were al-ready familiar with. For example, acting out a mathematical problem situation on the rug accesses parts of the brain that govern movement, vision, hearing, and social–emotional thinking; a worksheet could never accomplish this!

5. *Scaffold children to construct their own understanding.* The Early Math Collaborative is deeply committed to a constructivist approach. We see classroom teachers as experts who are more than capable of making instructional decisions, just like a good chef doesn't blindly follow a recipe. We also see young children as curi-ous and competent problem solvers who not only can, but will, solve the many mathematically based problems that abound in daily life. Spend an hour or less in the company of preschoolers, and you will hear all kinds of debate about Big Idea questions such as *Who has more? What's bigger?*—and the corollaries—*How much bigger? Is it fair?* Our role as teachers is to guide them—to frame and orchestrate problem situations in ways that take into account the remarkable developmental trajectory they can traverse.

At the same time, those of us who work with young children know how important it is to nurture their inborn instinct to question and problem solve. Worksheets and standardized measures are efficient—they look for right and wrong answers. Unfortunately, they also tend to bypass genuine understanding. Discussion—or maybe we should say good conversation—gives children opportunities to create and test theories, which is a powerful mechanism for the kind of learning that lasts and sustains new ideas. The Early Math Collaborative's approach to Big Ideas recognizes that rich discussion not only helps us develop understanding, but it is good evidence of what stage of understanding has been reached. Making your classroom a place where children enjoy sharing their ideas, both with you and with one another, takes time and a lot of patience, but the math-learning payoff can be enormous.

How Does This Book Introduce Big Ideas?

Each of the nine chapters in this text focuses on a small set of topically related Big Ideas. Table i.2 shows the relationship between the Common Core State Standards (CCSS) for Mathematics in Kindergarten and the chapters by topic.

For each topic, chapters have two main sections: ***Big Ideas*** and ***Implications for Teaching***.

- *Big Ideas.* At the outset of each chapter is a box that lists the Big Ideas for that chapter. Then, each Big Idea is presented and discussed one at a time, illustrated by examples from early childhood classrooms. Key words are highlighted to help you quickly get to the core understandings, and each Big Idea builds on the concepts of the one before it, helping you develop a rich set of connected ideas within the topic of the chapter.

TABLE i.2   Common Core State Standards for Mathematics in Kindergarten and Chapter Topics

CCSS Content for Grade K	Book Chapters
Counting and Cardinality	Sets Number Sense Counting
Operations and Algebraic Thinking	Number Operations Pattern
Measurement and Data	Measurement Data Analysis
Geometry	Spatial Relationships Shapes

• *Implications for Teaching.* This section focuses on planning classroom instruction to address the Big Ideas of the chapter. We compare and contrast different types of activities, discuss considerations for choosing materials, describe how to incorporate the Big Ideas into the routines of your classroom, and help you think about important math language you will want to use. We consider how young children's understanding of these Big Ideas grows as their capacity for generalizing matures, and we identify key points on the developmental trajectory. We also include suggestions for **Finding Great Math in Great Books**, as we believe that using a good book or story assures that children will be engaged and creates a shared experience that can be discussed and analyzed. Each chapter concludes with a **Video Link**—a connection to the companion DVD that shows teachers and children engaged in thinking about the Big Ideas. We include reflection questions to help you think more deeply about what you see.

Throughout the entire text, we include glimpses into the early childhood classrooms we know. ***Math Snapshots*** illustrate every Big Idea to provide a sense of how they look in a real classroom. ***Teacher Talk*** comments are woven throughout the chapters and share insights and discoveries from teachers the Early Math Collaborative has worked with over the years. We hope hearing from other teachers as they grapple with these new concepts will help you connect the Big Ideas to your own teaching.

The complete set of Big Ideas is presented in chart form at the end of the book and in an easy-to-print file on the companion DVD. We hope these ideas come alive for you and for the children that you teach!

Chapter 1

SETS
Using Attributes
to Make Collections

Big Ideas about Sets

■ Attributes can be used to sort collections into sets.

■ The same collection can be sorted in different ways.

■ Sets can be compared and ordered.

Math Snapshot

Ms. Simone is introducing a new bead lacing toy to a small mixed-age group of children in her preschool classroom. As she takes the lid off, the four children immediately start exclaiming over the shapes and colors they see. Tyra and Maria are excited by the sheer number and the colors; Jesse and Kyle, who are a bit older, notice how the tray breaks up the collection of beads into categories and look carefully at the different shapes. As soon as Ms. Simone gives the go-ahead, all four get a lace and begin pulling out beads.

We often fail to appreciate how much of young children's lives—and above all their play—involves thinking about and working with sets of things. A **set** is any collection that is grouped together in some meaningful way. For example, "my toys" are a set—the set of all the toys that are "mine" in contrast to the set that are Ruthy's. Or it may be a set of materials we find in the building area: a set of unit blocks on one shelf, a set of bristle blocks on another, and a set of well-worn plastic bricks on a third. In fact, in order to learn the names of things, children must create sets in their mind, like the set of "dogs" that includes their own dog, the neighbor's dog, and that dog that barks at us on the way to preschool. For their definition of "dog" to be like that of the adults around them, they must group these three animals together mentally to create a meaningful collection.

Sets, then, are basic to children's thinking and learning. However, they are also basic to our number system. One of the most important jobs of each number is to describe "how many" there are in a set of things—be it one, seven, or three hundred and nineteen. Before we can figure out how many apples there are, we have to decide which things are apples, and which are not. Once we've created the set of things that are apples, perhaps by separating them from the oranges, then we can count them. Counting requires a set, and as a result, the properties of sets have a large influence on the number system, and on mathematics.

For this reason, children in a math-rich early childhood classroom will have many experiences working with sets, including matching and sorting items, as well as combining, comparing, and ordering sets in different ways. They will need many opportunities to sort and categorize features of the classroom and to join in conversations about meaningful or useful ways to break a collection into sets. These experiences help them construct the ideas that are the foundation upon which competent and flexible counting can be built.

We have identified three Big Ideas that are the foundation for understanding the mathematical topic of sets.

- Young children who understand the first Big Idea, that *attributes can be used to sort collections into sets*, have a working knowledge of what a set is and how it is constructed. Experiences with attributes are central to developing this Big Idea, as they give a solid understanding of how we define collections of things.

- When young children are exposed to the second Big Idea, that *the same collection can be sorted in different ways*, they gain a deeper understanding of the relationship between sets and sorting, and the idea of a set becomes more flexible for them.

- Children who are aware of the third Big Idea, that *sets can be compared and ordered,* know that organizing things into groups makes it easier to figure out what we have more and less of.

Keeping these three Big Ideas in mind, you can ensure that the children in your classroom will develop a basic understanding of sets. That will lead in turn to enhancing their ability to think about and use not only sets, but also patterns and numbers—that is, to begin a lifetime of doing mathematics meaningfully. In the pages that follow, we describe each Big Idea in more detail. We conclude the chapter with implications for teaching.

Big Idea: Attributes Can Be Used to Sort Collections into Sets

Math Snapshot

Tyra, one of the youngest in Ms. Simone's class, exclaims, "There's lots and lots, at least one hundred teen!" She immediately grabs a few handfuls at random and starts concentrating on getting the beads onto the lacing string. "I'm going to do the mostest!" she announces.

As Tyra collects her share of beads, she shows she is thinking about "how many," since she mentions a large number name ("one hundred teen") and calls the set she will "do" the "mostest." Ms. Simone understands that Tyra's focus on quantity rather than on organizing the beads by category is developmentally appropriate. Still, she seems ready to start looking at **attributes** like color and shape and to begin to **match** items that are fully alike. Ms. Simone can play **Find My Match** activities with Tyra using a smaller collection of beads—for example, four hearts and four stars, with two of each being the same color. The game begins when Ms. Simone holds up a blue star and asks if Tyra can find one that is "exactly alike"—that is, both the same shape and color.

By keeping the variables such as number, color, and shape limited, Ms. Simone is helping Tyra focus on the matching problem, and is increasing her likelihood of success. At the same time, Ms. Simone structures the task to give Tyra many chances to *receptively* recognize a match before she suggests that Tyra actually *produce* one.

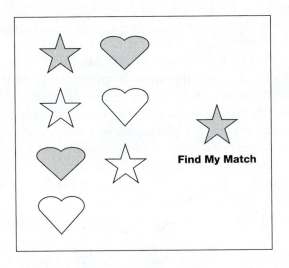

Find My Match

Over time, Ms. Simone can make this task more complex in several different ways. She can introduce more shapes and colors, increase the size of the overall collection, or, she can see if Tyra can figure out which one she *takes away*—can she find the one that doesn't have an exact match?

There are many opportunities to match items by a single attribute in early childhood classrooms, including many card and board games. However, the better you understand the Big Idea involved, the easier it will be to come up with activities that connect to children's everyday lives; just think of all the activities that might be done with pairs of socks, shoes, and mittens.

Sorting is different from matching because it involves reorganizing a whole collection, or set, into two or more subsets. As is typical of this early stage, Maria breaks the collection into two categories. She ignores shape, and focuses only on pinkness—all of the stars, butterflies, hearts, and other shapes can be separated into those that are pink and those that aren't. The mathematical term for what she does is a **binary sort** because she produces only two sets, one of which has the chosen attribute, and one of which does not.

Maria is ready to play **What's My Rule?** In this game, the leader separates out a set of objects that share an attribute that the rest of the collection does not have. Again, the game initially focuses on *receptive skills*, that is, the ability to *recognize* the rule someone else used to establish the set. So Ms. Simone might have the children watch as she separates out all the stars—whether red, yellow, pink, or blue—from a collection of 15 or 20 beads and ask "What's my rule?" This is much more difficult than **Find My Match**, because it requires that children ignore some of the differences between members of Ms. Simone's set so they can figure out what they all have in common.

What's My Rule?

Once they have experience in guessing Ms. Simone's rule, the children will be able to take over leading the game. Ms. Simone will say, "Who has another rule?" and let a child select beads for the rule-bound set. After observing a few times, this is a game she can move to a free play choice or math center.

One more way to give children experiences sorting collections is to do **People Sort**. In this game, rather than figuring out a rule, children apply a rule in a group setting with the teacher. To introduce the game, two hula-hoops or yarn circles are placed on the floor and a group of five children are called up. Initially, it helps to begin with a binary sort, based on directly observable attributes such as color of shirt, types of shoes, wearing glasses, etc. For example, the teacher might say, *I see five children in front of me. Some have curly hair* (points to one hoop), *and some do not have curly hair* (points to other hoop). The children then sort themselves into whichever hoop describes them, and the teacher encourages them (and the audience!) to talk about whether each set checks out.

This is a great activity because it involves the children themselves, using their whole bodies, something that young children always enjoy. More importantly, it provides a large-scale demonstration of how sorting works. Children who don't get the concept have a chance to figure it out while supported by their peers and the teacher. The point of this activity is not to understand the attributes, but to develop the children's familiarity with the sorting process and how it produces sets.

You will know that the game is successfully promoting mathematical understanding when the children are really communicating with you and each other about who does or doesn't belong in one hoop or the other.

Big Idea: The Same Collection Can Be Sorted in Different Ways

Math Snapshot

Kyle and Jesse like to work on things together in Ms. Simone's class. Kyle, who will be going on to kindergarten in a few month, has lined up the letter-beads to spell out his name. As he looks at them and the length of the lacing string, he shakes his head, "Just my name isn't enough; maybe I can separate the letter-beads with one of the fish to make it longer," he muses, adding, "cuz I go fishing with Pawpaw T."

In the meantime, his pal Jesse has four piles of different shapes he has pulled out saying, "I'm going to do a really tricky pattern: circle, star, fish, block, circle, star, fish, block." When Jesse hears Kyle say he wants to separate the letters of his name with fish, Jesse shoves over the pile of fish beads he has collected. "You'll need almost all the fish. I'll do butterflies instead."

Kyle and Jesse are typical of what happens as children gain experience; they soon move to sorts that involve more complex *attributes* that create more *sets*. When Kyle realizes that his name is not long enough to fill much of his lacing string, he selects another attribute and gathers another *set* of beads—in this case, fish-shaped. Jesse's **pattern** is also based on shape, but for his necklace, this attribute occurs in four different ways that create four distinct sets. To make his pattern, Jesse will select a single bead from the set of circles, a single bead from the set of stars, and so on.

When Jesse gives up his fish beads to his friend, he is not only demonstrating maturity, he is also on his way to realizing an important thing about sets: a single collection of items can always be sorted in more than one way. He sees that the fish beads can work as a contrast to his circles, stars, and blocks, but they can also be the "not-letter beads" for Kyle's necklace.

For young children this can be hard to understand, since it requires thinking about the many different characteristics of single items. That is, in one sort, a bead might be thought about as a butterfly, and in another, it might be considered pink. When children begin to understand this idea, they have learned something important about *same* and *different* that will help them become abstract thinkers and problem solvers in math.

Math Snapshot

Ms. Simone had called for a binary sort, with children who had white shirts in one set and children who didn't have white shirts in another. One boy hesitated and then moved into the white shirt hoop. Several children objected: "Teacher said just white shirts and yours isn't all white!" Pointing to white stripes in his shirt, he insisted, "I do have white in my shirt so I should be in this group." A little girl in a red blouse with white collar and cuffs then decided she should move over as well, leaving only one child in a green shirt in that hula hoop.

Ms. Simone recognized this was a good teachable moment and said, "I can see you children are really thinking. I can also tell I need to be careful about what I say. So let's do this again two different ways. First we will do shirts with *some* white and *no* white; then we will see how the groups change when I say *all white* shirts and *shirts that are not all white*." The children watched the sets go from four in the "some white" set and one in the "no white" set to two "all white" and three "not all white." They talked about how it was the same group of children, wearing the same shirts but that the sorting attributes had changed.

This scenario shows the children wrestling with two important ideas. First, they are noticing how carefully they have to define their attributes. The sort doesn't really work until everyone is clear about the specific thing that makes the two sets different. The fact that people have to negotiate, clarify, and agree in order to organize and create sets is an important real-world connection.

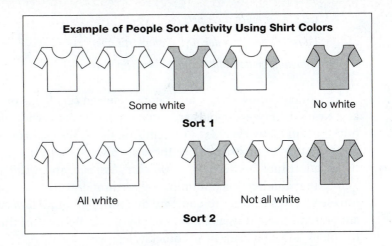

Example of People Sort Activity Using Shirt Colors

Some white　　　　　　　　　No white

Sort 1

All white　　　　　　　Not all white

Sort 2

Second, Ms. Simone structures the activity to help the children compare two different ways of sorting a single collection. In this way, the **People Sort** activity provides a very clear demonstration of the ideas that Kyle and Jesse had begun to explore in their thinking about how to use the fish beads. When ideas are this complex, the importance of multiple experiences can't be stressed enough. Over time, children will become more observant and their ability to think flexibly about attributes will grow.

Big Idea: Sets Can Be Compared and Ordered

Math Snapshot

Jesse runs into a problem. "There aren't enough block-shaped beads for me to finish my pattern." Kyle leans over the tray of beads and says, "Maybe you should use the use the little stars instead of the blocks—there are a lot more of them."

As soon as a collection is broken up into sets or groups, children and adults alike show a strong instinct to compare. Sometimes the comparison is about which set is "better," or preferred.

- *Cats make much nicer pets than dogs.*
- *I'd rather have wooden toys than plastic ones.*
- *The children don't like oranges for their fruit snack.*

Frequently, however, comparisons between sets focus on quantity, as Jesse's and Kyle's do. Five-year-olds are often especially concerned about the quantity-questions in many everyday problem situations: *Who has more? What's bigger? Is it fair?* Quantity comparisons like these are always about the three possible quantitative relationships between sets: *more than*, *less than*, and *equal to*.

Young children need multiple opportunities to see how sorting a collection into sets makes it easier to compare quantities. In our **Math Snapshots**, the beads are presented in a tray, already sorted by shape. Because of this, Kyle can compare the block and small star beads quickly, just with a glance.

But in real life, there are often situations where sorting into sets is needed before comparisons can take place. If we want to know whether more children brought their lunch from home or ordered a hot lunch, we would begin by sorting the children into two sets: the hot lunch set, and the cold lunch set. Sometimes even when the attributes are directly observable, like whether a picture was made with markers or crayons, sorting into sets provides the organization that makes comparison possible.

And when quantities are very close to equal and rather large, the only clear way to know which has more is to count. Comparing the nickels to the pennies in a full, mixed-up coin jar can be such a situation. And for our counting to tell us which there are more of, we must first separate them into meaningful sets. In a math-rich classroom, the teacher recognizes that questions about what's fair provide a natural chance to assess not only children's counting but also their ability to sort into sets.

As children become more competent at creating and manipulating sets, they are ready to sort and compare more complicated collections. An excellent activity, which can occur in either a small or large group, is **Shoe Sort**. Each child removes one shoe to create a pile in the middle of the rug. The teacher asks, "How can we organize this crazy pile of shoes?" and helps the group identify several sets into which the entire collection can be sorted.

Some classrooms may sort into "boots, sneakers, and other shoes" while others might focus on fasteners, and end up with "straps, shoelaces, and buckles." Once the sets are created, they can be lined up to compare quantities, and then placed in order from most to fewest shoes. This sort is different from a binary sort because (a) more than two sets may be produced, and (b) the attributes that define them are not opposites of one another (like pink and not-pink). We refer to this type of sort as a **multiple sets sort**. As in the **People Sort**, however, the **Shoe Sort** provides lots of opportunities for talking about how to define the attributes that make the sort work. It also helps children see how creating sets makes it easier to compare quantities.

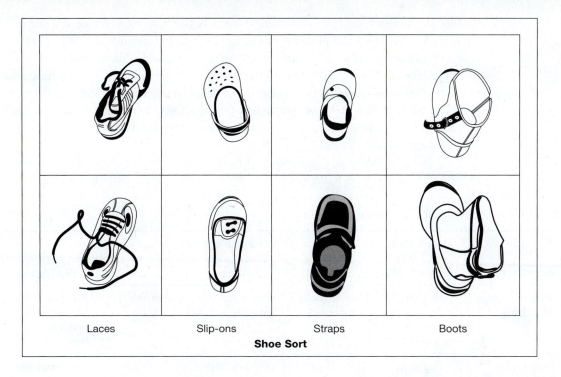

Shoe Sort

| Laces | Slip-ons | Straps | Boots |

It is important for the teacher of young children to know that ideas of more, less, and equal become more complicated when the items in the sets are of very different sizes or shapes. Which is more, ten raisins or two pizzas? Three elephants or twenty mice? Teachers can use comparisons like these to help children think carefully about number and its relationship to the real world. These ideas are difficult, and require teachers' help and clarification to point out that there are different ways to figure out "more" depending upon the kind of question we are asking. Creating a classroom that can support conversations about these concepts takes time, but it is extremely valuable for solidifying the ideas children have about both sets and counting.

Implications for Teaching

In this section, we focus on planning classroom instruction around sets. We describe which types of set-related tasks are more difficult than others, discuss choices about materials, and point out easy ways to incorporate thinking about sets into the everyday life of your classroom.

Developmental Trajectory for Set Understanding

We hope the stories from Ms. Simone's class made clear how thinking about sets is deeply foundational—it is the basis of our ability to name things, to categorize, to describe amount, and to make comparisons between groups. As we will see in Chapter 5, sets also make patterns possible. Clearly, understanding sets has far-reaching influence on a child's mathematical thinking and achievement.

We have also identified several different types of activities—like matching and sorting—that children need to experience in order to understand, create, and compare sets. To help you think about these types of activities, we have presented them in Table 1.1, and put them in a rough order by complexity. That is, less complex activities are presented first.

Table 1.1 is meant as a guide as you make instructional decisions—but you are the one who knows what works best for the children in your classroom.

TABLE 1.1 Activities for Exploring Sets

Activity Type	Description of Child's Competency	Example Materials	Example Classroom Activity	Teacher Talk	Big Idea(s)
Exact Matching	Recognizes total sameness to make an exact match	Pairs of socks or mittens	**Find My Match**	*Which sock is exactly like this one?*	Attributes can be used to sort collections into sets.
Sorting by a Single Attribute	Applies matching skills to make a set	Collections of objects that share some attributes but differ with others—like the beads	**What's My Rule?**	*That's right—I made a group of all the star-shaped pieces.*	Attributes can be used to sort collections into sets. The same collection can be sorted in different ways.
Binary Sort	Uses *one* attribute to change a collection into two sets using a yes/no rule	Observable attributes of clothes, appearance, etc.	**People Sort**	*If you are wearing red, step in this hoop. If you have nothing red, go to that one.*	
Multiple Set Sort	Uses one or more attributes to change a single set into many sets	Collections with varied attributes; natural materials or recycled goods such as bottle tops	**Leaf Sort**	*We sorted the fall leaves by color. What happens if we sort them by their shapes?*	
Compare Sets	Asks *"What's more/most?"* and may represent comparison with a graph or tally	Collections with varied attributes; sets that change over time	**Shoe Sort**	*What kind of shoes did we wear today? What if we sort our shoes on a rainy day?*	Sets can be compared and ordered.

For instance, if you tried the **What's My Rule?** game, and saw that some of them were really lost, it could be helpful to return to activities that emphasize **exact matching**. Similarly, children who are confused by an **open sort** such as a Shoe Sort may need more experiences with a simpler **binary sort**. So, too, you may feel it is important for the children to gain experience with many sorts before you focus on comparing the sets and representing "how many" with a bar graph or tally.

Make Sorting Playful

Teachers find that once they begin to think about it, their classrooms are full of natural opportunities to sort—many of them embedded in children's free play. In housekeeping, children are always sorting and categorizing as they rearrange the dress-up materials or set up supplies for playing store or restaurant. In other play areas, even best friends have to negotiate who gets how many of a certain kind of toy.

It is also true that every well-functioning classroom is organized. Materials tend to be stored in a sorted manner, simply for ease of use—the books in the reading corner, the easels by the sink, the duplos with the duplos, and the unit blocks with the unit blocks. This kind of organization makes it simple for teachers to mathematize the many ways that sorting and sets are part of the classroom, just by talking thoughtfully about it. Clean-up time is particularly packed with opportunities to notice and comment on sorting.

> **TEACHER TALK**
> Lynn, Head Start Teacher
>
> I have started taking time to make comments such as "Look what a careful job you two did putting the vehicles away. I can see you put them into different categories. You are even separating the big cars from the little ones." The two boys in that case just beamed. The next day, they came over to tell me "Ms. Lynn, we did it again. Maybe you can put 'Car Sorters' on the classroom jobs list!"

Help Children Define Authentic Problems to Explore Sets

> ## Math Snapshot
>
> After the beads had been in the classroom for a time, Ms. Simone challenged a small group of her 5-year-olds to come up with some new ways to sort the collection with its multiple colors and shapes into just two groups.
>
> It took a lot of exploration and discussion but eventually Kyle, Jesse, and Alix discovered they could separate the beads that looked like something real (butterflies, hearts, fish, etc.) from those that were simple shapes (rectangles, squares, cylinders, etc.). There was a fairly heated debate as to which group the stars belonged to—Alix thought they were "real" but Kyle insisted that they were a shape because real stars in the sky didn't look anything like that.

Ms. Simone's challenge illustrates a key factor in effective problem-setting: the question she asked was authentic and it was open-ended. Reorganizing the beads, either in the tray or perhaps into a few more convenient containers, is a teacher-directed activity that is intimately connected with the life of the classroom. In other words, Ms. Simone was intentional about a real problem that truly did have more than one possible solution; for example, the children could have decided to sort beads with curves from beads without curves, or those that were colored from those that were plain wood. Sorting for sorting's sake will not be as interesting or as powerful an activity.

Identifying and using attributes to sort, categorize, and compare sets involves a great deal of talk in Ms. Simone's classroom. The fact is, the development of mathematical thinking about sets goes hand in glove with the young child's increasing ability to name things and attributes, and, equally important, to raise questions.

Talking about the attributes of a collection as the children think about different ways to sort is a powerful way to increase vocabulary. Children will have strong preferences about whether or not they like things that are fuzzy, smooth, soft, or prickly. All children benefit from learning more "robust" words to describe things—and they delight in learning a new term that expresses a strong personal preference—or dislike. Words that help children organize their world make them better creators and users of sets.

Choosing Materials for Sets

It is not easy to select items that will engage and hold children's interest while presenting just the right level of complexity. When you are planning an activity focusing on sets and sorting, take time to consider the factors that can make the task more or less difficult, as shown in Table 1.2.

Recognize Receptive Understanding

Math Snapshot

Ms. Simone smiles and comments on Maria, who is concentrating on finding all the pink beads. "Look at you, Maria! I can see that you are looking carefully for just one color!" Maria smiles back and says, "Rosado! Good for la princesa!!" Ms. Simone agrees, "That's right, Maria, pink is a good princess color!"

TABLE 1.2 Materials and Sorting

Factor	Easier	More Difficult
Number of items in a collection	Sort 4 toy cars by color	Sort 20 toy cars by color
Number of attributes that differ between items	Sort into: • red bears • blue bears	Sort into: • small red bears • large red bears • small blue bears • large blue bears
Type of attributes	Sort red and blue mittens and gloves by color	Sort red and blue mittens and gloves by whether mittens or gloves
Number of kinds (ways in which a single attribute varies)	Sort a collection of • red and blue • gloves, mittens, and hats	Sort a collection of • red, blue, yellow, pink, and green • gloves, mittens, and hats

Young children will vary in their abilities to use spoken language. Some children are highly verbal, and will be able to use language to explain their thinking. Others may have more emergent language skills, and, thus, it is very important to pay careful attention to what the children are *showing* you they know, rather than *telling* you. This is also true if your classroom includes children who are English Language Learners. You will be able to identify all kinds of situations where they may understand an attribute but not have the vocabulary in English to express themselves. It is important to pay close attention to what children's gestures and actions indicate and to offer acknowledgement and feedback. Because Ms. Simone noticed that Maria was creating a set of pink beads, she was able to comment on it. This, in turn, encouraged Maria to use the language she has to name the set—a powerful experience every young child should have.

TEACHER TALK
Julie, Kindergarten Teacher

After years of teaching children who have English as a second language, I realized it's just as important to watch what children do as to pay attention to their words. Many of my Spanish-speaking students get mixed up with color names but they never have any trouble picking out items in their favorite color!! This gives me a strength I can build on.

Finding Great Math in Great Books

Once we recognize that thinking about sets is closely linked to sorting and categorization, it's easy to find books and stories to launch lessons. Here are a few of the Early Math Collaborative's favorites:

- *Five Creatures* by Emily Jenkins. The cover of this lovely concept book shows a young girl, her parents, and two cats who are featured on every page in it. However, each page spread also reveals different ways the five creatures can be categorized—from three humans and two animals (2 sets), to three who like milk, one who's allergic, and one who takes it only in coffee (3 sets). Not only is the book a great way to introduce doing **People Sorts**, but it also naturally invites innovations; sometimes a cluster of children will work with the teacher to write their own *Five Children at our Table*. Some teachers have sent home a book template with the title page "_____ Creatures in Our House" and encouraged families to complete the project for display on Family Night.

- *Shoes, Shoes, Shoes* by Ann Morris gets used in many of our classrooms to start a **Shoe Sort** activity. The brief text under Morris's wonderful multicultural photos invites conversation as it builds vocabulary about attributes and introduces many ways to sort. Morris's other *Around the World Series* books work equally well, including *Hats, Hats, Hats; Bread, Bread, Bread; Houses and Homes;* and *On the Go*.

- *Is It Larger? Is It Smaller?, Shapes, Shapes, Shapes,* and many other of Tana Hoban's books explore sorting attributes. Like Morris, she uses photos; however, Hoban's text is minimal to nonexistent, allowing children and teachers to have many rich conversations about how the items shown fit the title of the book.

- *Goldilocks and the Three Bears* and *The Three Little Pigs* are just two of the classic children's tales that incorporate sets and patterns throughout their plot structure, language, and details. As children return again and again to illustrated versions such as those by Jan Brett or Barbara McClintock, they will literally be able to see a wide variety of ways sets of things can be the same and different. Acting the stories out and doing extensions can enrich the process—as happened when a preschool classroom produced a child-illustrated book about things that might be found in The Three Bears' house. One child pictured large, medium, and small boots while another imagined the bears would need a big, medium, and small refrigerator!

- *"A Lost Button"* from *Frog and Toad Are Friends* by Arnold Lobel; *Are You My Mother?* by P.D. Eastman; *A Mother for Choco* by Keiko Kaza; and *Is Your Mama a Llama?* by Deborah Guarino are all preschool favorites that illustrate how a good story can revolve around a sorting problem.

In Lobel's story, teachers might use a collection of buttons to show why Frog had difficulty finding a button that had the exact attributes of the one Toad lost. The young ones in the other three stories use physical attributes to "sort" their mother from other animal mothers. Again, acting out these stories will help children literally play with sorting problems—and puppets, felt boards, or small collections of items can be incorporated into centers and free play options to keep the thinking going.

▶ Video Link

You may be working through this book on your own; or perhaps you are a member of a professional learning community wanting to explore how to enrich the mathematical thinking and learning in your early childhood classrooms. In either case, we invite you to watch the video called *People Sort* and then discuss or journal on the following points.

1. In what ways do you see this activity as open-ended and involving problem solving by the children rather than a rote, highly teacher-directed activity?

2. What kind of instructional decisions has the teacher made in terms of the logistics of the game? Discuss whether you would make the same decisions for your classroom or what modifications you might make.

3. What evidence do you see that the children are developing a better understanding of the Big Ideas about sets through this activity? What do they say, or do, that gives evidence?

Chapter 2

NUMBER SENSE
Developing a Meaningful Sense of Quantity

Big Ideas about Number Sense

▪ Numbers are used in many ways, some more mathematical than others.

▪ Quantity is an attribute of a set of objects and we use numbers to name specific quantities.

▪ The quantity of a small collection can be intuitively perceived without counting.

Math Snapshot

Ms. Flores is leading her preschoolers in a whole group activity. She passes out paper plates to each of the 18 children; some have dots and others have numerals. She calls on Julio to stand next to her and report what his plate shows. Julio's plate has the numeral 5 written on it. Ms. Flores asks everyone to look at their plate and says, "Anyone else with 5, please join Julio." Maria stands up, "I have 5 dots." She shows her plate with four dots at the corners of a square with a single dot in the middle, as on a die, and counts the dots for the class, pointing at each one in turn. "You have 5 too, Tito," Maria says. Tito stands up hesitantly and holds out his plate, which has a row of 2 dots and a row of 3 dots. Ms. Flores smiles reassuringly and says, "Can you count your dots, Tito?" He points and counts "1, 2, 3, 4, 5. But that's not just five, that's all the numbers!"

Historically, psychologists and educators have questioned the appropriateness of teaching numbers in preschool. Number is an abstract concept, and young children tend to think in concrete terms. Thanks to a great deal of recent research in cognitive development over the last 30 years, we now know that infants are sensitive to quantity and can make good quantity comparisons (more than, less than). Young children have more innate ability to sense quantity or set size than we previously believed. In fact, most children enter school with a wealth of *informal* knowledge about quantity that provides a strong foundation for number learning and understanding.

The transition from this innate, informal number knowledge to a conventional understanding of number sense is a major cognitive development that takes place gradually. When adults celebrate that young children can count to 10, 20, or even much higher, they typically mean that children can say the number word list fluently and in order. This is indeed an impressive feat for a young child who hasn't been talking for very long; nonetheless, that accomplishment does not mean that the child has developed a complete sense of number.

Tito in Ms. Flores' classroom, for example, can enact the counting procedure to 5, but does not seem to understand why his plate matches Julio's, which has the numeral 5 on it. Unlike Maria, who uses the counting procedure to determine how many dots she has, Tito has not yet coordinated all the moving parts that make the number system work. Counting his dots aloud does not yet connect for him to the *fiveness* of the set. Knowing the *number words* and *understanding their numerical meanings* are related but not identical accomplishments.

In mathematics, **number sense** is defined in a variety of ways. In this chapter, we define it as *the ability to understand the quantity of a set and the name associated with that quantity*. Strong number sense developed in the early years is a key building block of learning arithmetic in the primary grades, as it

- connects counting to quantities,

- solidifies and refines the understanding of *more* and *less*, and

- helps children estimate quantities and measurements.

In this chapter, we will examine the three Big Ideas that young children need opportunities to explore in their early years, so they can be competent users of numbers and operations in elementary school and beyond.

- Children who are aware of the first Big Idea, that *numbers are used in many ways, some more mathematical than others*, are beginning to understand that numbers are not always for counting or telling "how many." Awareness of this fact helps children sort out the confusing varieties of number-related input they receive in their daily life.

- Understanding of **numerosity** is central to number sense development. This mathematical term is explained as the second Big Idea: *Quantity is an attribute of a set of objects and we use numbers to name specific quantities.* When children gain deeper knowledge of this Big Idea, they know that when number words are used to name "how many," they describe amount, just as "red" describes color, and "hot" describes temperature.

- The third Big Idea reflects the way our brains are hard-wired to be attuned to numbers: *The quantity of a small collection can be intuitively perceived without counting.* Children are born with an ability to recognize sets of one, two, and three items, and with support, they can quickly name "how many" for collections of four, five, and sometimes more objects *without counting* one by one. Children don't need to be able to recite this Big Idea, but gaining experience with this kind of **visual number sense** empowers children and fosters a meaningful understanding of quantity, so it is important for you to be aware of.

Keeping these Big Ideas in mind, teachers like Ms. Flores provide many rich experiences throughout the day to build young children's understanding in number sense. We hope they will help you see many opportunities to help clarify confusions that young children may have about quantities and numbers. By focusing your teaching choices so that they illustrate these central concepts, your teaching about number can be part of a rich diet of meaningful activities that help children develop a solid and useful number sense.

Big Idea: Numbers Are Used in Many Ways, Some More Mathematical than Others

Math Snapshot

From 10 to 10:50 every morning, children are busy at the work of "serious play" that characterizes life in Room 105, Ms. Flores' classroom. A group of 3- and 4-year-olds chattering in English and Spanish in the housekeeping area are busy setting up a toy store. Micaela, Lisa, Tomas, and Julio are working on the vehicles they want to sell; they have arranged them in a line. Micaela says, "Let's put them in order, with the smallest one first." She places a convertible, and says, "I think this one should be first and be $1." Tomas points to the second vehicle in the line-up and says, "Well, this dump truck is the biggest, so it should cost $5." Lisa looks at the fire engine which is third in line and declares it should be second, since it is not quite as big as the dump truck. "Maybe it should cost $4?" she suggests as she moves it between the convertible and the dump truck. Ms. Flores looks at the $6 in her hand and thinks about which cars she can afford to buy . . .

Our number system is a work of great genius and practicality. It is both infinite and predictable. Because of its systematic precision and specificity, it can do more than describe amount or quantity; number words become useful names and reference points, allowing us to precisely identify places, objects, times, people, and spaces, both virtual and otherwise. As a result, numbers are everywhere in our life: time, temperature, telephone number, Social Security number, money, and test scores, to name just a few.

For this reason, a single numeral can mean different things in different situations. While 5 usually refers to that quantity that is one more than 4 and one less than 6, there are circumstances in which there is little if any quantitative meaning in the way it is used. Being the baseball player who wears the number 5 on your jersey does not mean that you always bat fifth, for example. In this context, 5 is simply an identifier. As children move through the world, much of their exposure to numbers will be in contexts in which they have little if any quantitative meaning, and this can cause children confusion.

For example, when we visit Ms. Flores' classroom, we look for Room 105. This room number is a **nominal** or **categorical number**, that is, a numeral used for identification only. While Room 105 may (or may not) follow Room 104 and precede Room 106, it is unlikely that it is preceded by a total of 104 rooms that begin with Room 1. If the building has a second floor, the 1 may stand for first floor, but this is not necessarily true. The number 105, in this case, is being used as a discrete identifier, or name. Like telephone numbers, television channels, social security numbers, zip codes, or numbers on sports jerseys, room numbers are not inherently mathematical. They do not indicate quantity, rank, or any other measurement.

When the hour hand on the clock points to 10:00, the children in Room 105 know it is "free choice" time. We call this a **referential** use of number, because it functions as a shared reference point. As adults, when we say "Let's meet at 4 o'clock this afternoon" or "Today is warm, almost 70 degrees," we understand that these numbers stand for something agreed upon by our culture. Like nominal numbers, numbers used as reference points are not inherently mathematical. Although we can rank or compare referential numbers (for example, 70 degrees is warmer than 60 degrees or 3 p.m. is one hour earlier than 4 p.m.), we usually do not engage in other mathematical thinking and operations about them.

In contrast to nominal and referential numbering, *cardinal* and *ordinal* numbers are building blocks for number sense and are essential for mathematical thinking. **Cardinal numbers** provide the answer to the questions *How many?* and *How much?* For example, when we ask the question "How many children are seated on the rug?" the answer, 18, serves as a cardinal number, telling us how many there are in the set of seated children. Understanding *cardinality* is a prerequisite to being able to meaningfully count or carry out number operations such as addition and subtraction.

Ordinal numbers refer to *position in a sequence*, as when the children in Ms. Flores' room point out which car is first, second, or third. When number words are used in this way, they do not indicate quantity; instead, they function as a new kind of name, one that specifies *rank or order.* Ordinal number words allow us to compare quantitative attributes and to say a particular doll is the second tallest in a collection of five, meaning that while another doll is the first in terms of height, this one ranks taller than the other three.

There is an enormous psychological difference between cardinal and ordinal numbers for young children. In general, there is an intuitive feeling that having *more*—a higher cardinal number—is better. Having 10 of something is definitely better than having 5, though 5 is better than 2. However, the reverse is true for ordinal

TEACHER TALK
Carmen, Pre-K Teacher

Timmy was one of those live wires you never forget!! I used to count out the order in which kids should line up, saying "You are 1, you are 2, and so on." One day I pointed to Timmy and said "You are 3." He fell into a rage, asserting, "I am not 3! I am 4! I am a BIG boy now!" He had his birthday the week before and he was still adjusting to a new sibling and the demands of being the big brother. I know children totally identify small numbers with age. So now I am really careful to use the ordinal form and say, "You are first, you are second, you are third, and so on."

numbers: being first is generally acknowledged as being best. We want to be first to make a choice of activity, first to cross the line when playing *Candy Land*, and above all, first in the hearts of important others. Being second or third isn't terrible, but being tenth is!

As young children are beginning to learn the cardinal and ordinal number names, they can easily get mixed up. Understanding that their confusion is a normal part of the developmental process can tune teachers into how a particular answer might reflect what is going on in children's thinking. Understanding where a child is coming from can also make it easier to clarify misconceptions. It also reminds us of the importance of providing clear and meaningful examples that really will help children develop a strong sense of the cardinal meaning of numbers.

 # Big Idea: Quantity Is an Attribute of a Set of Objects, and We Use Numbers to Name Specific Quantities

Math Snapshot

Ali, Tito, and Zandra are rereading *Goldilocks and the Three Bears*, looking carefully at the illustrations. "Look," Ali says, "here she's looking through the window. She doesn't see the bears—just the bowls." Tito, whose English is still emerging, points at each of the bowls in turn, first counting and then identifying the owner, the size, and then the color. "Uno, dos, tres; Papa-grandes, Mama-medianos, Bebe-pequeños!" Zandra turns the page and looks at the chairs. "One, two, three of them too! Look how big and hard Papa's chair is. I like Baby Bear's little rocking chair." Before they turn to the next page, Ali makes a prediction. "Now she is going to go upstairs and find the three beds!! One for Mama, one for Papa, and one for baby."

Children need many experiences and conversations to develop their understanding that when number words are used to name "how many," the numbers act as *attributes*. Thus all collections of three items have the attribute of being three in number, no matter how many other qualities they differ on. Three dogs are just as much as three chairs which are just as much as three bears or the three visible stars in Orion's belt. The term we use for the "threeness" of three is *numerosity*.

In order to understand the numerosity of a set, one must see past the qualities of the things themselves and see only **quantity**. Three is the quality that a set of three apples and a set of three crocodiles have in common. To see the threeness of the apples, we must set aside redness, shininess, fruitiness, roundness, and appleness among other attributes. In other words, you cannot find three in the physical world in the same way that you can find a rock or a dog; the **idea of 3** has to be constructed in your head, since it is a quality that we see best in *relationships between sets*.

Quantity is only one attribute of a set of objects. When Tito describes three bowls by saying "*grandes-azur; medianos-amarillo, pequeños-rojo,*" he identifies two other attributes of this set of bowls—size and color. Similarly, when Zandra talks about the *big hard* versus *little rocking* chairs that Papa Bear and Baby Bear use, she focuses on the attributes of size and type. Grammatically speaking, the number 3 here is an *adjective*, similar to other adjectives such as *red, big,* or *soft.*

Math Snapshot

In Ms. Flores' classroom, she is always careful to count **objects** with her children rather than simply reciting the counting words aloud—three apples, four girls, six crackers—using the number words as adjectives that describe a set. She also takes every opportunity to support mathematical thinking in her children. While listening to the conversation among Ali, Tito, and Zandra about Goldilocks and three bears, she asks the children if they would like working together to draw other sets of three things that they might see in the Bears' house; as she speaks, she holds up three fingers to emphasize the quantity. Ms. Flores' suggestion gets an enthusiastic response. One child draws three pairs of shoes, including sneakers, high heels, and hiking boots. Another draws three television sets. Ms. Flores' favorite is the set of three refrigerators—each a different size.

Repeated experiences connecting number words and numerals with the set of objects they describe has critical importance for the development of number sense. Sometimes, however, we use number names as nouns instead of adjectives, like then we talk about 3 as "the number which is 2 less than 5," or when we say that "two 3s make 6." This use of number names as *nouns* only makes sense when we are able to *abstract* the quantity. In Erikson's Early Math Collaborative, we joke about the use of numbers as nouns as being *naked numbers*–not appropriate for use with young children when they are just beginning to learn about them! Young children whose basic number sense is still developing need more experiences with the *adjective* form of numbers, in which numbers are named in context with the set they are describing, as in "four *children,*" "two *dogs,*" or "three *ice cream cones.*"

The distinction between using numbers as nouns or as adjectives is something many parents and teachers are not aware of. In their eagerness to increase children's level of achievement, parents and teachers sometimes bombard children with naked numbers, or drill children on the answers to $1 + 2, 2 + 3, 4 - 2,$ or other simple arithmetic problems. Because these numbers have been stripped of the stories and problem situations that make them meaningful, such drills end up as unengaging rote exercises that don't invite the important conversations that are essential for making sense. While sometimes children are advanced, and make connections to abstract numbers and symbol systems on their own, when adults push children to these ideas, it can cause confusion.

It is important to point out that while the *numerosity*—the quantity of things in the set—stays the same in all languages, the number names and numerals we use are arbitrary—they change from language to language. For example, in English *three* is the **number name** that is *tres* in Spanish or *san* in Chinese. **Numerals** are symbols we make on paper. While much of the modern world uses Arabic numerals such as 3, 5, and 106, the ancient Romans used III, V, CVI, while the Mayans used a system of dots and bars. Both number names and symbols are cultural tools that we use to help construct and understand the world in mathematical terms.

There is another complication: English Language Learners can be easily confused by number names and their homonyms: *one* is the same as *won*; *two* could be *too*, or *to*. Many children, even native speakers, have trouble distinguishing the /th/ sound in *three* and /f/ in five and may not hear the difference between 13 and 15. Furthermore, *thirteen* may sound very much like *thirty*, and *fourteen* sounds like *forty*. For all these reasons, it is helpful to be very careful to always have children *count something*, rather than reciting the number words alone. When you count something, the number words are presented in context, alongside additional information; this makes it easier for young children to sort out what is meant.

Math Snapshot

Mimi is in her second year in Ms. Flores' classroom, speaking both Spanish and English fluently. Before she started, her mother had died within days of being hospitalized with a stroke.

Mimi was a good student but early on Ms. Flores noticed that she never said "six" even though she seemed to be able to accurately count to 20. When she mentioned this to Mimi's father, he sighed and said, "It's odd because she says it in Spanish but she won't do it in English. I guess it's just one of those quirky things she does since her mother got sick and died."

Just as he said that, Ms. Flores realized that "six" and "sick" sound very much alike while the Spanish word for sick is "enfermos," which doesn't sound anything like "seis," the Spanish for six. The next time Mimi skipped "six," Ms. Flores remarked that this is a funny word in English because when you say it quickly it sounds like "sick" but if you say it slowly you can hear the "sss" sound at the end of the number and the "k-k-k" at the end of "sick." Mimi just looked at her and didn't say anything. But later that same day, Ms. Flores overheard her clearly and emphatically counting 1, 2, 3, 4, 5, **6**!! And Mimi has been saying six ever since!!

Big Idea: The Quantity of a Small Collection Can Be Intuitively Perceived without Counting

Math Snapshot

This week Ms. Flores introduces a new kind of materials—black sticker dots. As an introduction, she reads Donald Crews' book, *10 Black Dots*, in which the illustrations show 1 to 10 dots as different parts of a picture. For example, eight dots are used as the wheels on a large truck.

Sitting with a small group of children, Ms. Flores encourages children to arrange four black dots as many different ways as they can on a piece of paper. She adds, "You can add a few lines between the dots to show what you are thinking of." Tito points to his arrangement, "I make a four, cuatro!" Ms. Flores smiles, "Look at that, Tito, you used four dots to make a number 4! You have three in a line and then the fourth one a bit by itself!"

"Mines is two ghosts with eyes because 2 and 2 is 4," Ali explains. Ms. Flores nods and shows two fingers on each hand, saying, "You're right, Ali—2 and 2 make 4."

"I did my four in a straight line," Lisa explains. "It's like buttons for a snowman."

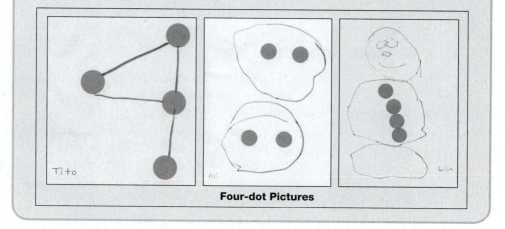

Four-dot Pictures

All children are born with an innate ability to perceive the difference between one and two objects. With support and experience, they can quickly perceive and name "how many" for collections of three, four, and five objects. This mathematical ability is called **subitizing**. From a Latin word meaning *suddenly*, the term refers to the ability to "see" a small amount of objects and know "how many" there are instantly without counting.

Researchers such as Doug Clements talk about two kinds of subitizing. **Perceptual subitizing** occurs when the number of items is three or less. Even very young children can rapidly identify a collection as having one, two, or three items, without counting. When the number of items gets a bit larger, as in four, five, or six, **conceptual subitizing** can help children know "how many" without counting. For example, the usual configuration of six found on dice or dominoes is sometimes perceived as two threes. When counting by ones is not used, but the subitizing

TEACHER TALK
Melissa, Preschool Teacher

I always thought it was important for children to "count to check." Now I realize that visual recognition of small quantities is part of children's number sense, and that if I always insist on counting, they might think it's not OK to just "see" a small number. When kids recognize a small quantity now, I sometimes comment that they "just know it!"

is not just a one-step process—that is, *see the two threes, combine the two threes to make six*—we call the process conceptual *subitizing* because the subitizing is combined with the understanding that *two threes make six* to derive the answer.

Not all arrangements of the same number are equally easy to subitize—preschoolers will recognize that there are five dots quickly if they are arranged like the corners of a square with a dot in the middle, but may be slower or less sure if the five dots are in a straight line, particularly if they are very close together. Two colors can be used thoughtfully within a set to create smaller, more easily subitized sets that will prompt children to use conceptual subitizing (as in two green and two purple).

While it's important that teachers get to hear children count out loud (as we will discuss further in the next chapter), it's also important that they acknowledge when children correctly identify a small quantity without counting it at all. Since we always want children to have multiple ways of finding an "answer" in mathematics, teachers of young children need to help children see that counting works, but that sometimes we don't even need it!

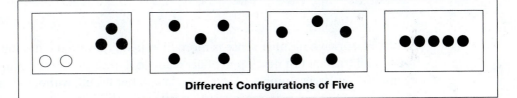

Different Configurations of Five

 # Implications for Teaching

As we have seen, children bring an intuitive quantitative sense with them on their first day of preschool. Through instruction and experience with quantities, children become familiar with numbers and develop a reliable mental picture of how they relate to each other. The role of number sense in mathematical learning is sometimes compared with the role of phonemic awareness in reading. In order to understand how to read, a child needs to understand how sounds work together to make words. In mathematics, children have to understand *threeness, fourness*, and how they are different from one another in order to become proficient in operations and problem solving.

Start with Small Numbers

Math Snapshot

At the parent–teacher conference, Micaela's mother spends some time reviewing the artifacts in Micaela's portfolio. She then asks whether the work is too "babyish" for her daughter. "Micaela can count to 100 in English and in Spanish, so why are you doing all these activities where the numbers never get above 10 or 20?" she asks.

Ms. Flores warmly agrees that Micaela is a very bright 5-year-old. "Still," she adds, "even very bright 5-year-olds don't make real sense of 'how many' 20 or 30 actually represents. Just the other day, Micaela was describing her grandma's birthday in your house. When another child asked her how old her grandma and grandpa were, Micaela said, "I think Abuelita is kind of like Mami and Papi, maybe 36. But *Abuelito (or Papito)* is really old, like 100." Her friend nodded in agreement and said that her grandfather was really, really old also, and then confided, "He had 1,000 candles on his birthday cake!"

Micaela's mother can't help laughing, "I suppose my father is a lot more formal than my mother, but I won't dare tell him this story!"

Ms. Flores is laughing also, but she explains what this story says about young children's number sense. "While Micaela can rote count much higher, we can see she doesn't realize that your parents need to be more than a few years older than you are. It's clear; neither of the children really knows how many 100 or 1,000 are. The fact is that saying the number words is different from understanding the quantity. Micaela will have a much easier time understanding the big numbers if she knows the meaning of small quantities well."

As Ms. Flores says, number sense is more than just knowing the number words. Young children are not developmentally ready to make sense of the numerosity involved in larger numbers. Like Micaela and her friend, without some kind of visual, concrete anchor, most 3- and 4-year-olds think of collections of 20 or more as "a lot." Since they are clear that numbers like 100 and 1,000 are treated by others as "big numbers," they fall back on using them to express how many are in what they understand to be a large quantity.

All the time Ms. Flores spends working on small quantities like 3 or 5 and not beyond 10 is meant to ensure that their understanding for larger numbers develops from a strong foundation; activities that take advantage of young children's innate subitizing skills and build their visual number sense will help them generalize their understanding that number names indicate a specific fixed quantity. They need to be clear that while the *size* of six elephants is much bigger than six mice, the number of animals or "numerosity" of each set is the same.

Link Numbers to Objects, Actions, Ideas, and Symbols

When working on numbers, Ms. Flores realizes that developmentally it is of critical importance to give the children many experiences in which they *represent* numeric meaning in different ways. Although she usually starts with *concrete manipulatives* such as dried beans, cubes, and crackers when she introduces a new number to children, she does not stop there. To understand five, for example, she makes sure that her students not only can show the meaning of five by counting out five cubes or drawing five circles, they also know the *numeral 5* can be used to represent the quantity.

Representations of number in Ms. Flores' mind are not limited only to manipulatives and numerals. She also uses sound and movement to put awareness of number into the children's eyes, ears, hands, and toes. At circle time, she might beat the drum five times and ask students to tell how many. During snack time, she will clap her hands five times to indicate how many goldfish crackers each student should have for the first round. On the playground, she might ask all children to jump five times before they are set free to run around or chase each other.

Teachers who have a good grounding in mathematical understanding like Ms. Flores know that number sense does not develop in a linear fashion, moving from concrete materials to pictures, and then to symbols. Rather, children learn best if there is a dynamic flow: thus, at one point, you can hold up a written numeral such as 5 and asks students to get five of anything to match the quantity it represents. Other times, show a picture of five circles and ask them to bring back the same *number* of objects; those who are clear about "fiveness" might bring back five blocks, pencils, or books.

In addition to concrete materials, pictures, and symbols, teachers and children have two other natural yet powerful tools—language and gestures. In Ms. Flores' classroom, one constantly hears conversation such as the following about numbers. "Tito, tell me how many beans you have here." "Cinco." "Cinco what?" "Cinco frijoles." "Wonderful, you have five beans here, but how do you know it?" "Yo cuento como, cero, uno, dos, tres, cuatro, cinco," Tito points to beans one at a time as he counts. "You count one by one. That's great! Is there another way to show me that there are five beans here?" Such a question could prompt a child to use a single hand to put a finger on each bean (if they know they have five fingers

TEACHER TALK
Amanda, Preschool Teacher

All my children can count to three and beyond, so I thought number arrangements with three would be too simple and boring for them. Was I wrong! After they made "three museums" with craft sticks, bottle tops, connecting cubes, and stickers, they were excited to point out the groups of three they saw in the classroom and around the school. Now that we are working on arrangements of four, they are starting to notice groups of four. I can see how building a deep understanding of these smaller numbers is going to help them when they get to bigger numbers and arithmetic!

on each hand), or to separate the beans into a pile of two and a pile of three (if they know that when they combine two and three, they always get five). Helping children see that there are different ways to determine how many beans there are is a great way to inspire mathematical discussion and flexible thinking about number.

As critical as they are in mathematical learning, concrete materials, pictures, and numerals in and of themselves do not automatically generate mathematical understanding. It is language that surfaces the mathematical meaning associated with manipulatives, connects concrete materials or pictures to symbols, and draws children's attention to foundational concepts or skills.

However, it is also true that an exclusive focus on language around number can trip us up. For many adults there is an assumption that *saying* something is equivalent to *understanding* it. Thus, children are discouraged from using their natural, concrete number tool: fingers. Using fingers to count or to show quantity is seen as a crutch. However, all we have learned from cognitive developmental research tells us that linking number concepts to the use of fingers, hands, and gestures is an important and powerful way to support learning and facilitate understanding of mathematical concepts. Helping children learn to use these constantly available tools to support their thinking will make them more efficient math learners down the road.

Consciously Address Visual Number Sense

Math Snapshot

Ms. Flores is using the dot cards while children are waiting to wash their hands for snack. She flashes a card with four dots in front of Tracy, who quickly holds up four fingers. Ms. Flores shows the card again and asks, "Do your fingers match the dots?" Tracy looks at the dots, looks at her fingers, and nods. Ms. Flores says, "All right, go get in line for the sink," and moves on to the next child on the rug.

This dot routine is just one example of how intentional teachers foster young children's visual number sense—that is, their ability to form mental images of quantities. Visual number sense builds on networks of sensory connections, enables children to picture and manipulate numbers in their head, and gives them a strong reference for many mathematical problem situations calling for estimation and measurement.

Dot cards, like dice and dominoes, are engaging tools to build number sense. Initially, you can focus on dice patterns for the numbers from 1 to 6. Gradually, introduce different arrangements of the same number to increase children's pattern recognition skills and use of visual part–part whole strategies. At times you might add color to spatial pattern activities, for example, by creating a four-pattern consisting of two red dots and two yellow dots. So too, five-frames and ten-frames encourage children to focus on spatial patterns for visual number sense by reinforcing those combinations of dots and empty spaces that add up to five and ten.

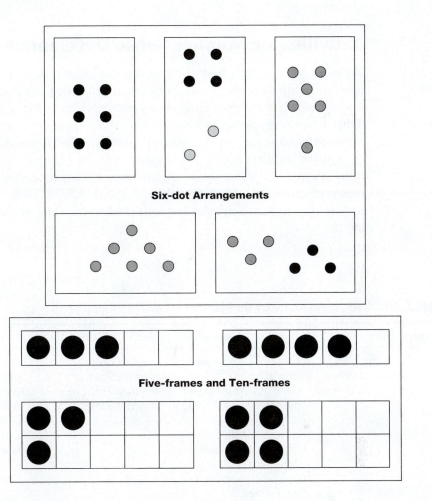

Six-dot Arrangements

Five-frames and Ten-frames

Build a Sense of Magnitude

Once children know the sequence of number words up to 10, it can be helpful to focus on developing their understanding of how numbers relate to one another. Knowing that six is more than four and less than nine is an important part of a useful understanding of what six is. Short number lines, from 0 to 10 (or 20 with older children), can really help children keep the sequence in mind. Eventually, children need an internalized number line, to support their own "mental math" involving the addition and subtraction of small numbers. Activities that ask children to identify "which is more" with small quantities will help them organize their thinking about magnitude, or relative amount. Such activities, however, tend to use numbers as nouns instead of adjectives, and so should be enacted after children's understanding of cardinal amount is relatively solid. In all cases, it is important that language, gesture, and a connection to a meaningful cardinal amount are integrated into these activities so that children become conscious of the relationship between what they see and their conceptual understanding of the quantity.

Activities for Number Sense Development

Table 2.1 lists activities that will help you implement the strategies we have identified to support number sense. For each activity, the table points out the key understanding the activity emphasizes and provides an idea for adapting the activity, depending upon your classroom's needs. These activities are not listed in a developmental sequence, since the understanding of different aspects of number develops in parallel fashion. It is the coordination of these different aspects of numbers that result in a strong number sense. Remember: focus on small numbers such as three and four first, ensuring that children have ample opportunity to develop a truly meaningful and robust understanding of these important building blocks.

TABLE 2.1 Games and Activities for Number Sense Development

Aspect of Number	Activity Examples	Key Understanding	Ways to Adapt
Connecting number words to objects, actions, ideas, and symbols	***Give Me a BIG 3 and a little 3*** For Big 3, children call out three of something very large (e.g., three elephants) or shout three times, and then something very small (e.g., three ants) or whisper three times.	Emphasizes number as an attribute of a set; emphasizes the *cardinal* understanding.	Use a large visual display of a single numeral accompanied by dots to reflect the quantity, so children can associate a visual representation and a symbol.
	Number Scavenger Hunt Children are asked to find a specific quantity of the same thing (e.g., one child brings back three pencils, another three dolls . . .).	Gives children a fun opportunity to demonstrate a *cardinal* understanding; links number name to objects.	Provide children with a "number card" with the number of dots or a numeral (or both) and have them take that with them on the scavenger hunt. Children can use this to "check" their work. All children can have the same number card, or they can have different quantities to collect.

(Continued)

TABLE 2.1 Games and Activities for Number Sense Development *(Continued)*

Aspect of Number	Activity Examples	Key Understanding	Ways to Adapt
	Making 10-Frames Tell students a number and ask them to place dots in 10-frames. Emphasize that while dots can be placed in any configuration, it is easier to see the total if the frame is filled systematically—completing one column or row before using the next.	Children create sets of the appropriate amount, emphasizing cardinal understanding; links to visual number sense activities using dot cards below.	Provide models of 10-frame cards for 1 through 10, and have children copy, making one card for each number to create their own complete "set."
Developing a visual number sense	***Name That Number*** Show dot cards or fingers quickly and ask child to name the quantity without counting.	Emphasizes *identifying* visual representations amounts.	Let children be the leaders, showing dot card or fingers, or naming quantities.
	Match That Number Call out a number and ask children to match with fingers or dots before getting in line.	Emphasizes *creating* visual representations of amounts.	With numbers greater than four, ask children to count the visual set to be sure.
	Dot Card Games Use quick-flash dot cards based on twos, fives, tens, doubles, or various arrangements and ask students to name/match the quantity.	Helps children who can already name small amounts presented visually to use this strategy in more complex ways. Leads to beginning understanding of number composition.	Focus on a single number, but present dot cards that emphasize different groupings, such as two blue and three red, followed by one blue and four red, for five.
Building a sense of magnitude	***Number Line Jump*** Draw a number line on the floor, marking one end with 1 and the other with 10. Give 10 children paper plates, each with a numeral and associated dots (1–10). Call numbers out of sequence (2, 8, 5, etc.), and work as a group to arrange children along the line one at a time.	Helps link cardinal understanding and the number sequence, enhancing children's understanding of how discrete numerals relate to one another.	For a less advanced version, call out the numbers in order, building the line as a group. For a more advanced version, call out a single number, such as 2, and have the child with that plate try to find her place on the line with supported discussion. Then have her sit down so that the "number line" is empty, and call out the next number.

Finding Great Math in Great Books

There are an enormous number of children's books about number, and new ones are being published every year. While some are mediocre, many are wise and inventive. The key to identifying better number books is to look for illustrations in which numbers are meaningfully associated with objects or events so that cardinal amount is emphasized—and of course it helps if the book is fun, beautiful, or otherwise engaging! Below are a few wonderful titles that can be revisited again and again to develop children's strong number sense.

- *Anno's Counting Book* by Mitsumo Anno offers one of the most effective ways to open up a conversation with children (as well as adults) about the multiple uses of number. The book is wordless but the illustrations call for constant conversations and discoveries about all the ways numbers get used. On the page marked 5, for example, we see the clock tower showing the time as 5 o'clock (referential) and the train is marked with 5 (nominal). But the train engine is pulling five freight cars through a landscape that has five evergreens and five leafy trees (cardinal). The little settlement has five buildings, and five children are playing. The list goes on and on. By the time we get to the last page, marked 12, we realize that the pictures have taken us through the calendar year as well as the numbers from 0 to 12.
- *Ten Black Dots* by Donald Crews is a standby in many mathematically rich classrooms like that of Ms. Flores. It invites wonderful creative expression extensions with a mathematical twist.
- *Count and See* by Tana Hoban brings together photos showing the designated number of objects on one side of a page, while the numeral and the corresponding number of dots are shown on the other. To extend the book, invite children to find photos in magazines or in the classroom archives that show sets of three or four or another number of things.
- *Splash* by Ann Jonas invites children to see how the number of creatures in a pond changes, according to who jumps—or is pushed in and who gets out. This is also a good book to use as a model for a classroom book.

▶ Video Link

In the video clip *Number Arrangements*, the preschool teacher gives children the opportunity to create small collections of three, four, and five with manipulatives such as cotton swabs, craft sticks, and connecting cubes. The video shows excerpts from the fall and from the spring because this activity was woven into the math curriculum throughout the school year. As you watch, consider the following questions:

1. What do you think the children gain by working at such length with small numbers?

2. Comparing fall to spring, what evidence do you see that the children's number sense has deepened?

3. How could this activity be part of your curriculum—not as a one-time activity but as a routine that children can return to again and again?

Chapter 3

COUNTING
More than Just 1, 2, 3

Big Ideas about Counting

- Counting can be used to find out "how many" in a collection.
- Counting has rules that apply to any collection.

Math Snapshot

Ms. Kami knows that rituals around seeing who is present and absent each day offer a wonderful opportunity to strengthen the children's sense of community in her blended classroom of 4- and 5-year-olds. Each child is standing at an assigned spot around the edge of the rug. Ms. Kami announces, "We will begin our count of who is here today with Ayla." The children join Ms. Kami in saying, "One child is here today," and Ayla sits down. Tony is on her left as the group chants, "Two children are here today," and then he sits down. So it goes around the circle until the count comes around to Asia, who is to Ayla's right and the only child left standing. Everyone joins in a triumphant, "Seventeen children are here today!!"

As Asia sits and takes her place "criss-cross applesauce" in the circle, Ms. Kami announces, "We have 17 children at school today. And we have 17 children in our class. So how many children are missing today?" Many children call out together, "Zero!" and everyone joins Ms. Kami in doing a Perfect Attendance Round of Applause.

There is no question that everyone delights in hearing young children count. The children themselves love the pattern and rhythm of the language as they chant or sing their way from 1 to 20 or 30 or even 100. They are warmed by the smiles and words of approval and admiration from important adults, just as the important adults, parents and teachers, take satisfaction in this demonstration of the beloved child's competence—the ability to count.

Counting is a part of young children's daily life. They love to count everything from the stairs they climb to the crackers they eat. But what is counting? What is there to be understood about counting? What do most children know about counting? What more is there to be learned? Counting seems very simple, but it is really quite complex. By developing a sophisticated sense of what counting is and what kind of counting we ought to emphasize in teaching, parents and teachers can better assist children with the development of counting skills and mathematical thinking.

There are two types of counting: rote counting and rational counting. **Rote counting** involves reciting the number names in order from memory. If a child says, "1, 2, 3, 4, 5, 6, 7, 8, 9, 10," the child has correctly counted up to 10 by rote. **Rational counting** involves matching each number name in order to an object in a collection. If a child says "one apple, two apples, and three apples" while tagging one apple at a time, the child has developed rational counting skills up to a certain number.

While accurate rote counting has its place in the process of learning to count, its function is rather limited. In contrast, when young children develop rational counting skills, they are armed with a tool that enables them to understand the concept of numerosity, to compare quantities of different sets, and eventually to engage in operations. Rational counting is a foundation for children's early work with numbers.

We have identified two Big Ideas teachers and adults should focus on to support the development of children's rational counting skills:

- The first Big Idea—*Counting can be used to find out "how many" in a collection*—speaks to the purpose of counting. Why do we count? We count because we want to know the quantity of a collection. And the collections can be physical objects (for example, chairs, apples) and nonphysical objects (for example, sounds in the room, ideas).

- *Counting has rules that apply to any collection*—this is the second Big Idea in counting. The four basic rules are *stable order; one-to-one correspondence; order irrelevance,* and *cardinality*. When a child applies these rules to a counting activity, he has mastered rational counting skills.

Big Idea: Counting Can Be Used to Find Out "How Many" in a Collection

Math Snapshot

Ms. Kami routinely has a Question of the Day for children to answer upon arrival at school. She always structures the questions for a yes or no answer, such as, "Did you wear a jacket to school today?" Each child has a clothespin with his or her photo glued on it, and they all clip the clothespins to a YES/NO T-chart to show their answers to the question.

One of the favorite classroom jobs in Ms. Kami's classroom is to be one of the two **Counting Captains** who serve for a week. One captain counts the YES responses, and the other captain counts the NO responses. At the end of the morning, Ms. Kami confers briefly with them, helping them count up the clothespins and record the number. Before dismissal, the Counting Captains report to the group how many responses in each column.

How much? and *How many?* are fundamental Big Idea questions that are so embedded in our everyday life that we often are not conscious that in fact we are doing math. We think of counting the children on the bus at the end of a field trip as a safety issue; or our focus is on balancing storage space and our family's eating habits when we calculate how many juice boxes, yogurts, or cans of soup we want to stock up on during a sale.

Knowing or understanding "how many," however, is a complex developmental process, which is closely related to the development of number sense discussed in Chapter 2. Recall, there are four different ways we use numbers in our daily life: referential, nominal, ordinal, and cardinal. Finding out how many is the **cardinal use of numbers**—the primary purpose of a counting activity. Knowing how many enables children to carry out number operation activities meaningfully. For example, children can compare sets (e.g., *here are three apples and two peaches—there are more apples than peaches*) and identify equivalence (e.g., *you have two crackers and I have two crackers, we have the same*).

Counting to know how many is also closely tied to children's **subitizing skills**—the ability to perceive a small amount of objects and know "how many" there are instantly without counting, which were discussed in Chapter 2. A goal shared by subitizing and counting is to find out how many. They differ by method: subitizing does not require a sequence of steps, whereas a highly structured set of coordinated actions is the very core of counting. With or without elaborate procedures, the goal is the same.

Subitizing can play a supporting role in the development of children's cardinal understanding. By naming small sets with numbers, children eventually connect that a set of three that they can instantly recognize, for example, is both *three* and counted by enumerating *1, 2, 3*. Imagine a child who can subitize three objects and who can rote count to three, saying *1, 2, 3* in the correct sequence. Each experience counting a set of three provides the child the opportunity to use what he knows—*there are three*!—to figure out how counting and cardinality works.

Another connection between number sense and the ability to find out how many by counting relates to the concept of **numerosity**. As you will recall, the concept of "threeness" has little to do with the particular objects that children are counting. That is, when counting a set, each number name (*one*, *two*, or *three*) is not attached to any particular object, at least not in a permanent way. The number names are used only temporarily, as a method of being sure each item is included in the count. In fact, these relationships between number names and particular objects are so temporary that they can be switched around without causing any problems, so that the object that is "one" the first time you count can be "two" the next time, and you will still get the same overall result.

This temporary naming idea is a rather abstract and alien concept for young children. Most of children's experiences with names tie them specifically to one item, or a particular set of items. *Mommy* is not any woman but the one who loves you and takes care of you daily. *Chair* refers to a kind of furniture for people to sit on, and can't be applied to the table without confusion. The counting words are different. They are used whether children count themselves, stuffed animals on their bed, shoes they wear, or crackers they eat. Further, we can count not only physical objects, like jelly beans, boys, and girls, but also actions, like hugs or kisses, sensations, like sounds and smells, and ideas, like wishes and imaginary friends. Numerosity is such a powerful concept that it can be applied to literally anything!

Last but not least, similar to number sense development discussed in Chapter 2, counting to find out how many relates to children's **concrete experiences**. That is, counting has to be meaningful to young children in order to make sense. For example, counting out four meatballs to place on one's plate during lunchtime is much more interesting and meaningful than counting to find out how many stars are printed on a worksheet. The former connects to children's personal interest whereas the latter is detached from their needs. Similarly, counting physical objects is easier than nonphysical objects, because it is less abstract. Repeated experiences with four meatballs, four crayons, and four toy cars provide the right input to help young children generate a meaningful understanding of *fourness*!

 ## Big Idea: Counting Has Rules That Apply to Any Collection

Thanks to TV shows like *Sesame Street*, many children enter preschool chanting or singing the number names from 1 to 20. Learning to count meaningfully requires both memorizing arbitrary terms or number names (rote counting) and rule-governed counting (rational counting). As described earlier, rote recitation of the number words is not the same as having a good number sense for what 20, 25, or 100 means. Experts agree that **rational counting** takes place only after children have mastered four key principles or "rules" of counting: *stable order, one-to-one correspondence, order irrelevance,* and *cardinality.* Each principle builds on understandings developed in the previous ones.

Stable Order Principle

Math Snapshot

After a group activity that involved counting and moving at Family Night, Danny's dad pulls Ms. Kami aside. "I noticed Danny was right in there with all the motions; but after 10 he was just saying random numbers like *two-teen, seventeen, five-teen, nineteen!* Should we get some flashcards to drill him at home so he doesn't get behind?"

Ms. Kami smiles reassuringly. "There's nothing to worry about. The more Danny hears the number words in the right order, the better he will learn them. But flashcards aren't nearly as effective as you counting things with him. Make a kind of game of it. Since you live on the second floor, count the steps as you go up and down. Count how many red cars you see in oncoming traffic. Or just for fun, count how many fingers or toes you have as a family."

The definition of the **stable order principle** seems obvious to those of us who have been counting for many decades: *Counting words have to be said in the same order every time.* The order—*one, two, three, four*, and so on, is fixed, meaning that *three* is always after *two* and before *four*. When Danny says *two-teen, seventeen, five-teen*, it is clear he has not mastered the **stable order** rule in counting. As Ms. Kami suggested to Danny's dad, repeated practice through games and daily experiences will help him develop both the understanding and the skills.

Because the order of number names is conventional, memorizing the sequence is a prerequisite to the use of the stable order rule in counting. However, understanding the stable order rule is more than just the rote recitation of the number sequence. Mathematical structures and patterns are embedded in the process of the rule's applications.

First, no matter what word or symbol we use to designate a quantity, *each number is always one more than the number before it and one less than the number after.* That is, the number sequence we use has an embedded mathematical structure. In terms of number sequence, three is always after two and before four. With regard to its mathematical structure, three is always one bigger than two and one smaller than four. Rote counting alone won't help to reveal this mathematical structure, but having the words in the right order makes their cardinal amount meaningful.

Number sequence also includes many interesting patterns that are central to our understanding of numerosity and place value. As you can see on the Hundred Chart illustration, our Arabic numerical system is base-10, or based on a system of 10s. Because we group numbers by 10s, we can represent all numbers using 10 digits (0 to 9), and there are patterns to how numbers are represented. Because of these patterns, we know that when we reach a number

1	2	3	4	5	6	7	8	9	10
11	12	13	14	15	16	17	18	19	20
21	22	23	24	25	26	27	28	29	30
31	32	33	34	35	36	37	38	39	40
41	42	43	44	45	46	47	48	49	50
51	52	53	54	55	56	57	58	59	60
61	62	63	64	65	66	67	68	69	70
71	72	73	74	75	76	77	78	79	80
81	82	83	84	85	86	87	88	89	90
91	92	93	94	95	96	97	98	99	100

A Hundred Chart

that has 9 in the 1s place, the next higher number will end in 0, and have a decade one digit higher. In this way, the fixed order of the digits 1 through 9, combined with our place value system, creates a fixed, predictable, meaningful, and powerful system.

It is well known that the teens in English are the one decade whose number names distort the pattern—while twenty-one, twenty-two, and twenty-three follow the pattern (name of decade number + name of ones-place number) with satisfying consistency, *eleven, twelve, thirteen, fourteen,* and so on sound like a random string. This is why Danny gets confused when he starts counting teen numbers. The Hundred Chart can be useful to help children, particularly kindergarteners and older, see how the number pattern *does continue* through the teens while practicing the stable order rule. For example, children can clap and say each number in the 1 to 9 sequence but jump up and shout at each 10 while looking at the Hundred Chart—and if it is not clear why we say *fifteen* instead of *five-teen* (or even *teen-five*), at least the numerical representation on the chart makes sense.

TEACHER TALK

Florence, Pre-K Teacher

I have found that the rhythm of a child's voice often indicates how confident he or she is about counting. Some children will fall into the counting chant from 1 to 10; in the teens you can hear some hesitancy and stop/starting. They may pick up the chant again for the 20s and 30s; but then at 39, they stop; sometimes after a pause they remember that 40 is next and sometimes they just get stuck.

One-to-One Correspondence Principle

Math Snapshot

Ms. Kami has been very thoughtful about working meaningful counting activities into the routine of her classroom. At snack time, each table of five has a Snack Chief. Whoever has the job for the week is responsible for putting out the correct number of paper plates or napkins, putting out the snack dish and taking the drink orders. Ms. Kami knows that this is excellent practice with one-to-one correspondence.

At the same time, Ms. Kami tends to use snacks that come in munchable bits like goldfish crackers or pretzels. When everyone is seated, one of the Counting Captains rolls the magic number cube. It is marked with dots; the faces are 3, 3, 4, 4, 5, 6. Once the Counting Captain has counted the winning die face and announced the result, the snack bowl starts its way around the table, with each child counting out the designated number of treats. Ms. Kami reports that the whole table joins in monitoring and helping everyone get a "fair share."

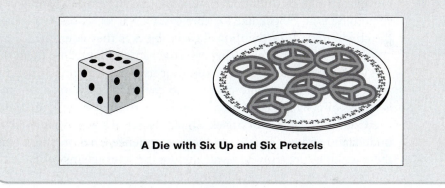

A Die with Six Up and Six Pretzels

Most of us are clear about the fact that the **one-to-one correspondence principle** means that *one number is named for each object*. While the principle seems obvious to adults, it does take practice and time for children to fully grasp it. That is, the child has to learn to coordinate the number words with the physical movements of a finger and the eye along a line of objects, matching one number word to one object until all of the objects have been used up.

In the process of developing one-to-one correspondence, young children often make three types of errors: (1) sometimes children tag each object one at a time but say the number words incorrectly, either missing words altogether or getting them out of order; (2) sometimes children tag certain objects more than once, also called double tagging; and (3) sometimes children miss tagging some objects, as shown in the following illustration.

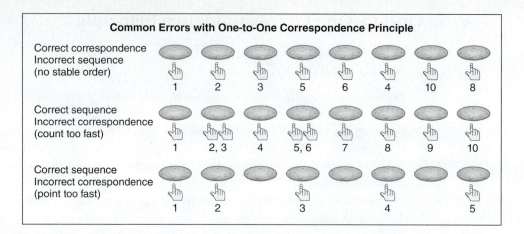

Common Errors with One-to-One Correspondence Principle

To help children develop the one-to-one correspondence principle, teachers with strong mathematical understanding like Ms. Kami are very intentional about making sure that all counting activities are linked to *counting something*—including movements like the Full Body Count routine she used at Family Night. When that something is an object, like toy cars in a line-up or goldfish crackers, she reminds the children to *tag* by pointing at each object as they count it.

When children are making an error, rather than telling them they are wrong, Ms. Kami asks them if they are sure—or uses opportunities when two children arrive at a different total to get them to check. In Ms. Kami's classroom, counting is always directly linked to an authentic situation, such as daily routines and jobs like Counting Captain or Snack Chief. Ms. Kami knows that children will better understand and use one-to-one correspondence when the problems are real to them and they are truly motivated to get the "correct answer."

Order Irrelevance Principle

Math Snapshot

It's another morning in Ms. Kami's classroom, and time to count how many children are here. Ms. Kami says, "Today we will start with Asia. One child is here today . . ." but before Asia can sit down, Ayla speaks up. "Yesterday I was the one child, but today it's Asia. We won't get the right number if it's Asia."

The **order irrelevance principle** builds on the rule of stable order and further generalizes the idea behind one-to-one correspondence. It can be defined as *no matter in what order the items in a collection are counted, the result is the same*. Children who fully comprehend the meaning of counting realize that rearranging the group of objects does not affect the total. Unlike reading, in which we go from left to right, it does not really matter whether the counting procedure is carried out from left to right, from right to left, or from somewhere else, so long as every item in the collection is counted once and only once. Children who understand the order irrelevance principle also understand that the number words are applied only temporarily to the object being counted and have nothing to do with the objects themselves.

This principle reflects the reality that in the world around us, most collections we want to count are scattered every which way so that we need a system to mark which items have been counted and which have not. Common strategies include:

- As each item is counted, it is pushed into another pile.
- A mark is put next to the items that have been counted.
- With a very large collection, items might be sorted into clusters of 2s, 5s, or 10s—those friendly numbers that we can easily skip-count.

Children's mathematical understanding has to be at a certain stage of development before they themselves begin to use one of these strategies. However, just as it is valuable to have the number sequence in long-term rote memory before full number sense is established, it is important to have model strategies so they seem natural when the child knows to use them.

Thus, Ms. Kami purposefully does think-alouds when doing any of the many counting tasks that teachers are responsible for. When counting children during circle time, she purposefully starts from her left side one day, her right side on another day, and from a random point on a third day. When seeing a small collection of cubes on the table, she counts one by one and drops the cube into a basket. When counting up money for a field trip, she might say, "Children, will you thank your parents for me. Everyone sent in dollar bills instead of coins so I can easily count how much we have. I'm putting all the $5s together in this pile and that one is the $1s." Children standing nearby chime in as she puts the stack of bills in her hand and lays them down as she counts—first the $5s by fives and then the singles by ones.

The order irrelevance principle helps children develop flexible thinking skills. They gradually learn that there is more than one way to count a set of objects and there are many useful strategies that make counting scattered objects easier.

Cardinality Principle

Math Snapshot

Today there are no children absent. As a group, when they get to the last children to be counted, the class chants ". . . 15, 16, 17." Ms. Kami always follows up the process by asking, "So how many children are here today?" When the children respond "17" she knows they understand that the last word used in a counting sequence tells you how many are in the set.

As simple as it might seem, understanding cardinality actually involves two different uses of number: first, the child applies the numbers to the objects being counted, using the correct number sequence (stable order principle) and counting each item once and only once (one-to-one correspondence principle). Second, once the count has finished, the counter reuses the last number word she said during the count to name the total amount of the set. In this way, the final number name is different from the earlier ones in that it not only "names" the final object and signals the end of the count, but also tells you how many objects have been counted altogether.

When a child counts, there are a number of ways that we can find out whether the child has grasped the principle of cardinality:

- When asked, "How many altogether?" the child names the last number that was counted and does not need to count over again.

- The child can *count out* a specified number of items to create a set of given quantity. When asked, "Give me five from that pile of cubes," the child counts out five cubes and hands them over as a set.

- When given more items to add or subtract from a set, the child can *count on* or *count back*, instead of *counting all*. When told, "Sam had five toy cars and Nana gave him four more for his birthday, how many does he have now?" The child may need to count actual items of manipulatives but responds by saying, "So he had five and got six, seven, eight, nine—he had nine altogether."

- The child knows that the quantity remains the same despite of the fact that the arrangement of objects changes. For example, the child responds, "It is still five" when a linear array of five items is arranged in a circular pattern.

Once again, children whose primary experience in counting is "naked number" recitation of the number sequence are less likely to understand the cardinality principle and apply it to counting activities. Those who have experienced counting as an authentic and useful way to establish "how many" can make much more sense of number operations that call for joining, separating and comparing sets—the topics that will be explored more thoroughly in Chapter 4, Number Operations.

 Implications for Teaching

In many ways, number sense and counting are so closely connected it seems they should be considered together. However, over the years the Early Math Collaborative has come to a deeper appreciation of how complex the concept of *number* is and how important it is to allow young children to construct their understanding as they move back and forth from concrete to pictorial to symbolic representations of number. Thus, we devoted one chapter to exploring how humans come hardwired with an intuitive sense of *numerosity* or quantity for very small amounts. We looked at the importance of nurturing and building on that instinct in early childhood classrooms: we need to offer the children many engaging and authentic experiences that use the natural capacity for subitizing so that the children develop visual number sense.

In this chapter, the focus has shifted to conventional words and symbols that are used to represent numbers and to answer the essential question of *How many?* that dominates so many aspects of our daily lives. Indeed, counting is one of the earliest mathematical abilities that young children develop. There is strong evidence that children's mastery of counting principles at the end of kindergarten predicts their level of arithmetic abilities in the primary grades. To help young children master the counting principles, we suggest several teaching strategies to keep in mind.

Develop Rational Counting Skills through Authentic Experiences

Full rational counting with a strong grasp of cardinality up to 10 is a process that takes usually two to three years to develop. For most children, rational counting starts to show up at the end of preschool or beginning of kindergarten. In kindergarten, many children master good number sense to about 20 or 25. Developmentally, most kindergarteners and even some first graders do not have a precise idea of "how many" numbers over 50 and 100 really represent. This has some serious implications for teaching. *Overemphasizing rote counting to high numbers before the counting principles are established for small numbers is counterproductive.* It can completely blind an adult to the fact that a child who can count to 100 may understand "how many" only in quantities under 20 or 10.

To help children develop a strong foundational understanding of counting rules, it is critical to start with small numbers through many authentic experiences and mathematical conversations. The daily routines in the classroom are a good place to explore counting. Whether it is taking attendance, making sure there are enough smocks in the art center, or seeing how many snacks there are, it is important to provide authentic opportunities for children to count. Table 3.1 is a list of activities that can be used to support the development of the four counting principles in young children.

Counting activities that include movement or other cues literally put the odd/even or the 5s and 10s structure of the number system into children's eyes, ears, and bodies and thus firmly fix them in long-term memory.

TABLE 3.1 Activities to Support the Counting Principles

Principle	Evidence/Skills	Activities and Routines
Stable Order	Fluency in counting using number *names* correctly first by 1s, then skip-counting by 2s, 5s, and 10s Knows number sequence forward and backward—can continue an "interrupted" count	• Counting songs and movement/games • Counting up and back from any number • Posting and referencing a 1–10 number line that uses dots plus numerals
One-to-One Correspondence	Coordinates saying one number word with one point to each object	• Daily routines such as in snack, passing out this or that, and lunch tickets • Music/movement games such as marching to a drumbeat • Board games with paths to move along by counting spaces
Order Irrelevance	Arranges and rearranges a collection to confirm count Groups objects for more efficient counting	• Starting counts of a fixed set such as taking attendance beginning with different children • Using think-alouds and modeling using a system such as lining up, clustering, counting by 2s, 5s, or 10s
Cardinality	Labels small sets by quantity (with or without counting) Counts out a given number Counts on (or back) from a given quantity	• Label the cardinal value of a set after counting (*1, 2, 3, 4 . . . 4 books*) • Routines that involve counting out a specified number such as snack (*4 crackers and 2 slices of cheese*)

Use Routines to Practice Counting

Math Snapshot

Shortly after the winter holiday break, Ms. Kami introduces a new attendance system. She has arranged 20 peel-and-stick library pockets in two lines on a poster board. Each line features five red pockets and five white pockets. In front of the poster, a can holds 17 wooden sticks, one for each child in the class.

Ms. Kami explains that when the children arrive each morning, they place one wooden stick in any pocket on the chart. At group time, she brings out the chart and the can, which has two sticks left in it, since Becca and Dagan are absent, and asks, "Does anybody have any ideas about how we can use our new chart to figure out how many children are here today?" A number of children have suggestions and Ms. Kami tries each one out with the group watching.

"Just count the pockets with sticks in them," Jane says. As Ms. Kami points, the children count to 15. "So how many children are here today?" Ms. Kami asks. Several respond "15" and Ms. Kami writes the number on the board.

"It would be easier to count if we put all the sticks in pockets next to each other and left the empty ones at the end," Danny says. Ms. Kami does that and the group again counts 15 sticks.

"I know it's 15 because there's 2 sticks left in the can," Chris shares, and Ms. Kami has him demonstrate. He pulls out the two sticks and counts up, "See, it's 15 up there and these sticks are 16 and 17. And 17 is all we have."

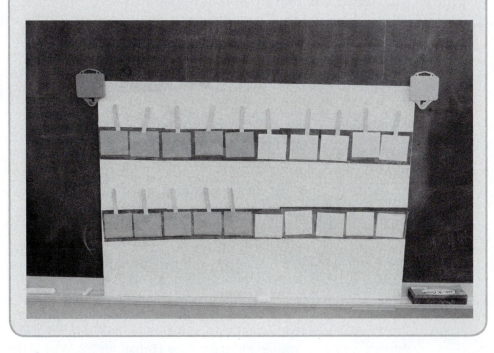

This new attendance routine that Ms. Kami uses for her classroom helps children practice the rules of counting in a number of ways:

- There are 17 sticks in the can; each child has one stick and every pocket can hold one stick—a clear case of *one-to-one correspondence*.

- The attendance chart has 20 pockets broken into 4 sets of 5 to strengthen children's visual understanding of how many, or *cardinality*, using the sets of 5s and 10s.

- Children can put their sticks in any pocket, which reinforces *order irrelevance*. The arrangement of the pockets embeds the idea that there could be a system used—and when children have developed sufficient understanding, they will apply it on their own, as Danny does with his suggestion.

- Chris's suggestion that they count up from 15 (the number of children present) to 17 (the total number of children in the class) is another instance of *cardinality* understanding. Fifteen names *the set* of children who are present. Chris starts with 15 and counts on two more for the two absent children, rather than counting from one again.

In addition to helping children master the counting principles through daily exercise, Ms. Kami also uses the opportunity to illustrate multiple ways to reach the same result. Such experience is fun to participate in and encourages children to think mathematically and flexibly.

Highlight Number Pattern and Structure to Advance Rational Counting Skills

For many adults, reciting numbers and the alphabet seem equal accomplishments. In fact, when the sequence has been committed to memory, the two feats are equivalent. However, there is a significant difference between the alphabet and the number sequence when pattern and structure are considered. Compare how quickly you can say what comes before and after

- The letter *H*
- The number 25

If asked what comes four places before or after H or 25, the difference in retrieval time is considerably greater for H than for 25. Why is that? That's because starting the alphabet with ABC is a convention; if the Greeks had begun with their letter string with *chi*, *rho*, *zeta*, we probably would be learning our CRZs.

While the ABC sequence is arbitrary, numbers follow a well-defined and predictable pattern. Once we understand the structure, we can continue accurately counting up or down from any amount. As well, our number system is a base-10 system. Each time we get to the next 10, we begin the sequence 1, 2, 3, 4, 5, 6, 7, 8, 9 again. Knowing such a pattern, counting big numbers become so much easier. Also, there are "friendly" numbers such as 5 and 10, which are easy-to-remember landmarks in our number system. Maybe because we have five fingers on each hand and 10 fingers altogether, children learn to group and skip count by these "friendly" numbers first. Counting games and experiences that integrate the number structure and patterns, such as Ms. Kami's attendance chart, not only help children with their counting skills but also advance their understanding of our number system.

The calendar routines that have become the staple of many preschool and Head Start classrooms are unfortunately not an activity conducive to children's number sense and counting skill. In the first place, the 7-column, 5-row grid gets filled in a different way each month, since the day on which the month begins and the number of days is highly variable. Even if that is not the case, 7 is a very "unfriendly" number—most people find it very challenging to count by 7s; it is an unnatural break in the 0–9 sequence of digits and does not invite use of our natural counting tools, our fingers and hands. The base-10 structure of our number system is completely lost by the calendar format.

Furthermore, for young children, psychological time, which is much more important to them than clock or calendar time, doesn't correspond at all to regular units like minutes, hours, days, weeks, or months. Though they may be able to rote recite or sing the days of the week and the months of the year, these units mean little if anything to young children. They are likely to feel they have to wait forever for their birthday next week; but if they are enjoying themselves, that same week seems to pass in no time at all. Children may know a song giving the days of the week, but be unable to answer or make sense of question such as "If your birthday is on a Tuesday, what day of the week is it before your birthday?"

The 10 to 20 minutes spent daily on calendar would be much more productive if teachers put the number structure and patterns into the children's bodies by including counting games, songs, and movement activities.

There are some alternative ways to do calendar in preschool that do help children see how the number of days in a month grows. Some find that creating paper link chains, with a new link added each day is an effective and engaging visual picture of the increase. Such calendars reinforces the **plus-one** structure of the number system. School day links can be made with one color and home days with another.

Others have found creating a linear calendar is effective. Each month, the teacher puts up a long roll of paper marked from 1 to 28, 30, or 31. Anticipated events like birthdays, field trips, and holidays are written in balloons above the date. If something special happens on a given day, that event is also entered. Each day a marker such as a large clip is moved to the next date. At the end of the month, the class reviews all that has happened in the month, so that it becomes a kind of classroom timeline. Teachers using this method report children develop a much stronger sense of time because the linear strip gives them a visual measure of how long it will be to an anticipated event as well as a concrete sense of what happened in the immediate past and what happened longer ago.

 ## Finding Great Math in Great Books

Every year a host of new counting books comes out. We can reference only a few here, so we have chosen ones that bring out the principles of counting.

- *One Gorilla* by A. Morozumi and *Fish Eyes* by Lois Ehlert are two great counting books that emphasize the plus-one structure of our number system. The illustrations increase children's engagement with these books. In addition, both name other attributes of the collections, helping underscore the idea that number is one of several possible attributes.
- *One Duck Stuck* by Phyllis Root and *A Frog in the Bog* by Karma Wilson are among some of the most appealing counting books that build a theme or story into the number sequence. In these books, children find it natural to use one-to-one correspondence to show how many are in each new set of creatures. The books also have delightful illustrations and rich language. There are a number of editions of counting songs that work in a similar way, including *Over in the Meadow*, which is available in several beautifully illustrated editions, and *This Jazz Man* by Karen Ehrdhart, which uses the traditional chant *Knick, Knack, Paddy Whack* to celebrate African American musicians.
- *Ten in the Bed* by Penny Dale or *Five Little Monkeys* by Eileen Christelow, *Ten, Nine, Eight* by Molly Bang and *10 Minutes till Bedtime* by Peggy Rathman are additional delightful stories and songs that emphasize the idea of counting on or counting back.

► Video Link

In the **Movement Counts** activity, the teacher first reminds children of the book *From Head to Toe* by Eric Carle that they have read together before. The teacher then leads a game with the whole class of children in which they move their bodies like the animals in the pictures of *From Head to Toe*. As you reflect on what the video indicates about counting, here are a few questions to consider:

1. What is the value of matching movements to counting words with one-to-one correspondence? What does such exercise do to English language learners?

2. Why is there a need to exaggerate each body movement in this activity?

3. Why is it important that teacher and children count aloud with one-to-one correspondence to the body movements?

4. What evidence do you see of children's understanding of the counting rules?

Chapter 4

NUMBER OPERATIONS
Every Operation Tells a Story

Big Ideas about Number Operations

- Sets can be *changed* by adding items (joining) or by taking some away (separating).
- Sets can be *compared* using the attribute of numerosity, and *ordered* by more than, less than, and equal to.
- A quantity (whole) can be *decomposed* into equal or unequal parts; the parts can be *composed* to form the whole.

Math Snapshot

Ms. Green's kindergarten class loves listening to and acting out classic childhood stories. Currently, they are exploring different versions of *The Gingerbread Man*. Whether it is the traditional tale, the Appalachian *Johnny Cake, Ho!,* or the Asian *Run-Away Rice Cake,* the same mathematical problem situation is embedded in the story: at first, the number of characters chasing the gingerbread person increases and at the end, there is definitely at least one character subtracted, thanks to the wily fox!

The story has been revisited often enough that Ms. Green is confident that everyone is familiar with the structure of the story. Today, Ms. Green plans to periodically stop the action and have the audience report on "How many now?" They will be considering how the number of characters on the stage for the big chase changes over the course of story.

In our discussion of counting, we have already talked about the difficulties young children have with making sense of "naked" numbers. Just as number sense develops when children are clear that *something is being counted*, the ability to make sense of number operations depends on the foundational understanding that *every operation tells a story*. Time and again, everyday life brings up compelling questions about *How many now? How many more or fewer?* and *Is it fair?*

Number operations are the tools we use to find the answers to these questions. When children focus on what happens when we join two sets together or separate a set into parts, they learn about how quantities change. When they have lots of experience comparing amounts, they become familiar with thinking about differences between sets. And when they have opportunities to see how a single large set can be composed of two or more smaller sets, they get comfortable with the fact that larger numbers contain smaller numbers. These ways of mentally modeling real situations in order to answer the questions *How many now? How many more or fewer?* and *Is it fair?* are what we mean by *number operations*.

In fact, in the early years, there is no need to focus on arithmetic and the symbols used to represent addition and subtraction. Just as children need many experiences with concrete, meaningful representations of "threeness" before they are ready to use the numeral 3 without context, they need many experiences thinking through how relationships between quantities work in the real world before they can reduce their thinking to the use of a plus or minus.

When adults rush to the memorization of rote facts such as 3 + 3 = 6, they may rob children of the opportunity to understand why the fact is true (or that it is true!). Before we ever introduce symbols to pull the mathematics out of the context, children need many experiences seeing that three friends and three more friends is six friends, that adding three apple slices to three apple slices gives you six, and that three pencils and three markers make six things for writing are needed. The symbols will come in time, and with greater understanding, when children have had many opportunities to problem solve and to develop their own strategies for doing so.

It is equally crucial that we give children multiple ways to make sense of a problem situation such as *How many now?*—by acting it out, making drawings, or using manipulatives. Rote mastery of all the ways to add and subtract the numbers 1 through 10 isn't much use when what children need to do is to identify what *the unknown* is in a problem situation, and have some plan for how to figure it out based on the *relationships between the numbers* that are given. Having a story to think about helps children visualize the problem situation; at the same time, it may provide more motivation to persevere to find an answer. Keeping number operations firmly grounded in mathematical problem situations involving the *changes*, *comparisons*, and *part/whole relationships* is the best way to prepare young children for later arithmetic. These three types of operations underlie the Big Ideas of Number Operations:

- Many problem situations involve change—adding to or taking away from a set. Such changes lend themselves to concrete models or to acting out as sets are joined or separated and then counted to find out *How many now?* However, it is also important for young children to make the more foundational generalization that *adding increases* and *taking away decreases* the quantity in a set. These understandings reflect the first Big Idea: *Sets can be* **changed** *by adding items (joining) or by taking some away (separating).*

- Other problem situations require comparing sets to answer the questions *How many more?* or *How many fewer?* The second Big Idea—*Sets can be* **compared** *using the attribute of numerosity, and* **ordered** *by more than, less than, and equal to*—helps children build the understanding they need to think about a set in relationship to other sets and begin to make comparisons between numbers. Familiarity with this idea prepares children to address questions they will encounter in first and second grade, such as *"If Ilan has 10 crackers and Juanita has 8, how many more does Ilan have?"*

- In order to figure out part/whole relationships within a given set, children must understand the third Big Idea: *A quantity (whole) can be* **decomposed** *into equal or unequal parts;* by the same token, *the parts can be* **composed** *to form the whole.* This understanding is a necessary foundation for operating on and with numbers. Children need to recognize that smaller numbers are contained in larger numbers and be able to describe the parts of numbers. When they can do so, they are building strategies that will later allow them to address a complex problem situation such as *"Junie has five pencils. Three of them were given to her by Marcos this morning. How many did she have before?"* That is, they need to be very comfortable with the idea that the quantity of five is not just a collection of ones, but can be thought of instead as a group of three and a group of two.

In all cases, the three Big Ideas emphasize *the relationships between numbers* in a problem situation. Helping children understand them deeply will lay a strong foundation for knowing that all operations tell a story—even when in later years, the story is only represented as symbols such as $4 + 2 = 6$, $6 - 5 = 1$, or $6 > 5$.

As children encounter mathematical problem situations, they develop a fairly predictable set of strategies for addressing them. At first, strategies for solving problems rely heavily on using concrete objects to model the situation and counting to find the unknown. Strategies like this, which involve a physical representation of the quantities in the story, are called **direct modeling** strategies.

Later in development, as children become more comfortable with the counting system, they begin to use numbers themselves as "stand-ins" for the things in the story. So rather than putting out two more counters to represent a situation in which two cookies are added to a plate with one cookie already on it, a child will say "the first cookie is one . . . two, three!" perhaps while holding up two fingers. Strategies like these, which require children to "double-count" ("two" is 1 more, "three" is 2 more than "one") are far more complex than direct modeling strategies, and are commonly called **counting strategies**.

In this chapter, we will spend a lot of time discussing the direct modeling and counting strategies children develop as they encounter joining/separating, comparison, and part/whole relationship problems. Teachers who can recognize these strategies, we believe, are better prepared to support their development in children's thinking. There are many different types of direct modeling and counting strategies, specifically tailored to finding the unknown in each kind of problem situation. For this reason, we have included a table (Table 4.1 on page 77) in the Implications for Teaching section of this chapter that organizes and defines them. We hope you will refer to this as you read through the Big Ideas section to support your own understanding of how these strategies work and what they look like.

Big Idea: Sets Can Be *Changed* by Adding Items (Joining) or by Taking Some Away (Separating)

Math Snapshot

In the version of *The Gingerbread Man* that Ms. Green's class is acting out today, the story line has been altered to make it a bit more complicated. At different points, the little old woman, the little old man, the horse, and the cow and three farmers join the chase. But then the little old man gets tired and drops out; soon after, the cow and horse get distracted by a pasture of green grass, and a bit later the farmers return to their fields. Only the little old woman is left to watch the Gingerbread Man accept the fox's fatal offer for a swim across the river.

At each point that the number of characters changes, Ms. Green freezes the action and asks the audience to describe what has changed on stage. For the most part, the children notice that the "stage" on the rug is getting crowded with actors and that the line of characters in the big chase is getting longer, and then shorter again. Some count by ones and announce the result. Some start from the last count and adjust the number based on the change described in the story.

All along, Ms. Green makes a stack of connecting cubes to match the number of characters throughout the story. Ms. Green asks the children to explain what happens to the number of characters in the story. "First it was just the little old woman and man chasing him and then the cow and the horse were more," Demarius explains, "but with those farmers there are lots more chasing!" Kayla points to indicate the stack of cubes and comments, "It went up and up and up and then down and down and down."

TEACHER TALK
Jayme, Pre-K Teacher

I have been working on getting the children to explain what happens when we add or take things away from a set. I was aware that English Language Learners can confuse the terms *more* and *less* or *fewer*, but many children whose first language is English do it too. So I've become really careful about using gestures, spreading out my hands to show *more* and bringing them together to show *less* or *fewer*.

In everyday life, the number of things we have or need often involves a *change*: we start with some and add more; alternatively, we might have a quantity and need to take some away. Young children may not keep track of the specific count, but they are sensitive to changes in quantities, expecting there to be more or fewer than before, depending on the action of the story.

As Demarius and Kayla's comments indicate, acting out the story with real people or with manipulatives allows them to literally see the change from *more* to *fewer*, or vice versa. The audience sees the set of characters grow, then shrink, while the actors have to adjust their positioning and movements as more characters join or separate from those on stage. Knowing that adding always increases, while taking away always decreases a set, lays the foundation for children to evaluate whether the number they arrive at in answer to *How many now?* makes sense.

In the earliest stages of strategy development, the first *direct modeling* strategy young children use to solve change stories is **counting all**. As each new chaser joins the pursuit, some children in Ms. Green's class always start from 1 and continue counting 1 by 1 until they reach the total number for that round. Similarly, a story that involves a decreasing change (for example, $8 - 2$) can be solved with the counting-all strategy; just count how many are left on the stage after two sit down! As more chasers join in pursuing the Gingerbread Man, Kayla adds connecting cubes; she counts that there are eight, then she *directly models* the action in the problem situation by physically taking away two to show the cow and the horse abandoning the chase; she then counts the six remaining cubes. In both cases, the strategy of *counting all* requires a concrete representation to "operate" upon, whether it is classmates acting out the story, cubes, fingers, or marks on a paper.

With experience, children eventually become more efficient and introduce a *counting strategy*—in this case, **counting on**. In Ms. Green's class, Tryce is eager to explain what she did when the three farmers joined the group: "*See, there's already five people, so the farmers are six, seven, eight—there's eight now.*" As she says the number words, Tryce holds up three fingers on one hand and uses them to keep track of how many to count on. This double count ("six" is 1 more, "seven" is 2 more, and "eight" is 3 more than 5) makes the counting-on (counting) strategy more complex than the counting all (direct model-

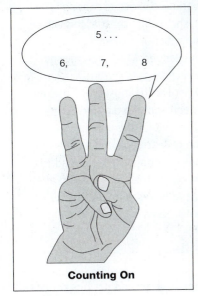

Counting On

ing), but it is also quicker, since not every object has to be counted to derive the answer.

At first children usually *count on* with smaller numbers, often ones they can subitize. Thus Tryce put up her three fingers automatically, without needing to count them; she then counts on—one by one using the other hand—to arrive at the total.

Surprisingly, *counting on* is also commonly used to solve separating situations. For example, when three characters leave a group of seven chasers, Demarius *counts on* to find out how many are still after the Gingerbread Man. He knows that three quit, so he raises one finger at a time and *counts on* from three until he gets to seven: "*Four, five, six, seven.*" As he looks at the fingers he has raised, he announces the total: "*So there are four chasers now.*" Demarius realizes that it is easier, and more reliable, to *count up to* the total in a separating story, than to *count back from* the total to find the answer.

TEACHER TALK
Adrienne, Kindergarten Teacher

I can see that children's number sense is really stronger once they start to use a counting-on instead of counting-all strategy. A few days ago, Tony came over to tell me that he didn't have enough scissors to pass out one to each child. He said he had 17 but he needed 25. I happened to have 6 scissors at hand and asked him if that would be enough. Tony started counting them, saying "I already have 17, so that makes 18, 19, 20, 21, 22, 23—I still need 2 more to make 25." Just a month ago, he would have had to count the full collection of scissors beginning with 1.

As children develop stronger number sense, they are able to *count on* without having to use their fingers or manipulatives. Once they have recognized that our base-10 number system is a pattern, they become less and less tied to counting one by one and begin to use more advanced counting strategies, including being able to *count on* or *count back from* any number. By the end of kindergarten, they are also likely to have a sense that number operations are basically efficient ways of counting.

Big Idea: Sets Can Be *Compared* Using the Attribute of Numerosity and *Ordered* by More Than, Less Than, and Equal To

Math Snapshot

Ms. Green has invited the children to work in pairs to make up their own Gingerbread stories to act out. Krystal and Kaiden have decided their story will use gingerbread twins—a boy and a girl—just like Krystal and Kaiden. Early on, the gingerbread twins split up and go their own way to the river with various characters chasing after each one. As Ms. Green helps organize the acting out, she recognizes that this will be a perfect situation to have the audience compare the number of characters chasing each gingerbread twin. At each point that the number changes, Ms. Green pauses the story to ask the audience to compare the number of characters chasing the gingerbread boy to the number chasing the gingerbread girl. For the most part, children count by ones and announce the total. One child has been appointed as recorder and writes the new total in each column, one for the boy and one for the girl.

At first it's the same: the little old woman and the cow are going after the gingerbread girl, while the little old man and the dog chase the boy. But Kaiden adds a herd of five horses to the boy's group while Krystal imagines three pigs chasing after the gingerbread girl. Daneeka answers, "The gingerbread boy is winning. He's got more people chasing him." Taylor adds, "The boy's got seven after him and the girl only gots five."

From early on, children visually compare sets to determine which set has more or fewer objects—think of the oft-heard protest at snack time, *"She has more than me!"*

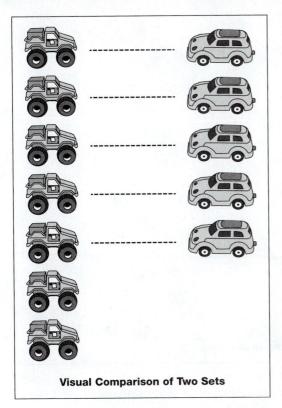

Visual Comparison of Two Sets

However, this visual comparison only works well when the sets being compared are either very small so we can subitize or of distinctly different sizes. Otherwise, we need to use numbers to calculate exactly *how many* more or fewer in one set than another.

The first strategy children use to compare is **matching**, which is a *direct-modeling* strategy. To model how two sets compare, children use concrete objects to represent each set and match them using one-to-one correspondence. For example, a child will line up seven toy trucks and five toy cars and be able to "prove" there are more toy trucks because its line is longer.

In the early years, children need many experiences with this kind of concrete comparison of sets. On one hand, it helps them develop a sense of the relative size of numbers, or their **magnitude**. They understand, for example, that 8 is quite a bit more than 3, but not much more than 7. At the same time, concrete comparisons help children realize that the matching comparison is being done in reference to "how many"—not to size. For example, four bowls take up much more space than six spoons (see page 72), but when you try to match them one to one, there are clearly more spoons. When one-to-one comparisons occur, they emphasize the numerosity of each set.

Most of the children in Ms. Green's kindergarten classroom have gone beyond visual matching (direct modeling strategy) to be able to make the comparison strictly in terms of numbers; Daneeka and Taylor are able to think, "I counted seven in one line and five in the other, and seven is more because seven comes after five when we count." On one hand, naming the total in each set is a function of understanding cardinality, as we discussed in the chapter on number sense. Comparing based on these totals, however, also calls for a good foundational grasp of what *ordinal* numbers represent. In mathematical terms, they not only can *compare* the number of items in the sets, they also can *order* them from first/most to last/fewest. In other words, **ordering** is another type of counting strategy in which the order of the number sequence determines the relationship between sets—one set can be *more than*, *less than*, or *equal to* the other in terms of quantity.

The ability to use ordinal numbers to make comparisons and state the difference develops gradually. Extensive experiences with subitizing, matching, and comparing will eventually lead children to create a "mental number line" in which they can compare numbers by their order in the counting sequence; that is, they learn to reason that if the counts of two sets are five and seven, the set

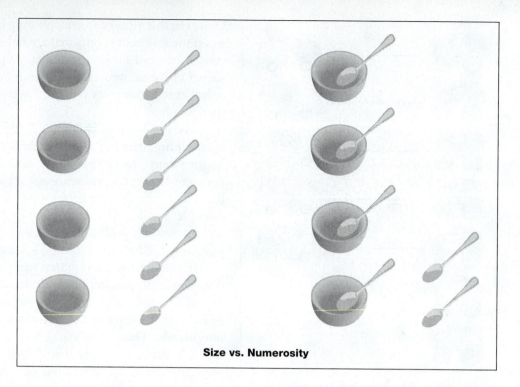

Size vs. Numerosity

with seven has more because seven comes later in the counting sequence than five. Once this mental number line is solidly in place, it becomes a simple matter to compare two sets without matching one-to-one when the quantity of each set is known, but this level of sophistication in thinking takes time and the right experiences.

Math Snapshot

Ms. Green uses Daneeka and Taylor's response to go beyond comparing the two sets to identifying the difference between them. "Yes, there are *more* characters chasing the gingerbread boy. Daneeka, do you have any idea of how we can figure out *how many* more?" Daneeka asks the children playing the five characters chasing the gingerbread girl to line up and then has the seven characters chasing the gingerbread boy form a matching line; she points to the two children in the gingerbread boy's group that are left over and reports, "He has two more."

Taylor offers a different way to show how many more. He points to the number line on the blackboard and says, "If I start at 5, it takes 2 hops to get to 7."

Finding out *how many more* (or *fewer*) calls for a step beyond simply comparing. When Daneeka matches the children one-to-one, and then recognizes that there are two more in one line, she understands that both groups include five, but to get to seven, you have to do two more counts in the number sequence. Taylor does the same thing in a more abstract way on the number line. In both cases, they are establishing that the difference between the five and seven is two.

As we already noticed, for young children, finding the difference does not necessarily mean subtraction. With both direct-modeling and counting strategies, children are likely to count up from the smaller set to the larger set. They are likely to think, *"How many more chasers would the gingerbread girl have to get to have the same number as the gingerbread boy?"* This *counting-up-to* strategy is the easiest to "act out" concretely with objects and supports children as they begin to construct their "mental number lines" on which to compare and order numbers. As we saw was true with change situations, it takes more time for children to confidently *count back from* the larger set to the smaller set to find the difference.

Big Idea: A Quantity (Whole) Can Be *Decomposed* into Equal or Unequal Parts; The Parts Can Be *Composed* to Form the Whole

Math Snapshot

The Gingerbread Man is just one of many classic tales that extend across Ms. Green's curriculum. In May, she introduces Alma Flor Ada's *Dear Peter Rabbit* that has a variety of the characters from the tales get together for a party. The children's excitement about this book leads to another math project.

Working in pairs or trios, the children are to plan a Fairy Tale Party. They will make a poster showing who is coming to the party—the total number of guests has to add up to 10. The poster will show the title of each story they include as well as the number of characters from that story.

Taylor, Krystal, and Tryce agree that they want Snow White and Seven Dwarves to come to their party, even if that takes up 8 of their 10 guests. "Let's say Cinderella and Sleeping Beauty are coming too," Tryce suggests.

Kaiden and Demarius want the Big Bad Wolf to come with the Three Little Pigs. "Then the Troll and the Billy Goats Gruff can decide to be friends too, and come," Kaiden says. Demarius is keeping count, "That's four and four, so eight so far—we need two more." "I know," Kaiden says, "Let's get the other Big Bad Wolf to come with the Woodchopper from *Little Red Riding Hood*."

As each group presents their posters, Ms. Green scribes a chart showing the different ways the number 10 is being composed.

Just as she did with *The Gingerbread Man*, Ms. Green builds a rich mathematical exploration into an engaging activity that draws on the power of stories for teaching and learning. The conditions she sets for the Fairy Tale Party are highly intentional. Ms. Green knows that all the children in class have basic number sense for 1–10;

but she also recognizes how important it is that they understand that any given whole number can be broken down into different parts. She wants to be sure that the children who glibly recite "5 + 5 = 10" are just as aware that 10 can be 4 + 6 as well as 2 + 2 + 2 + 2 + 2 or 1 + 1 + 8. Ms. Green draws sets of circles, one circle for each character. All the characters from a single story are circled to create a clear set and labeled with a numeral. She does not include the names of the "guests," because she wants to keep the focus on the numerosity of the sets rather than on the individual characters, and the children's posters can serve as a reminder of the particulars, if they are needed.

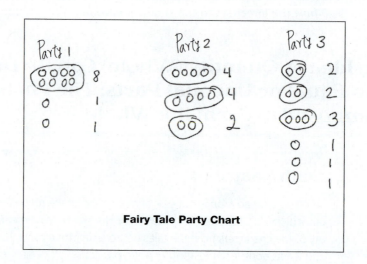

Fairy Tale Party Chart

In effect, *composing* and *decomposing* numbers up to 10 involves the conceptual subitizing we explored in the chapter on number sense. Well-established *visual number sense* for small quantities extends to larger quantities when children gain experience composing and decomposing numbers. When children know the parts of numbers and see how they relate to other numbers, they will be able to add and subtract with automaticity. For example, they will know that 3 and 4 must be 7, because 3 and 3 are 6 and 1 more is 7. Or they will know that 3 and 4 are 7, so 7 − 3 must be 4. It may be automatic, but this thinking is anything but rote. It is built on a deep understanding of **part/whole relationships**.

Problem situations with part/whole relationships involve a single collection or set—the situation is static. However, there is an *unknown* number that must be figured out in relationship to the others. The whole may be unknown: *There are two boys and six girls. How many children in all?* Or, one part may be unknown: *There are eight children. Two are boys, and the rest are girls. How many are girls?* While there is no action like there is with change situations involving joining and separating, children develop the same type of strategies—*direct modeling* and *counting*—to find a solution. With direct modeling, children *count all* using objects, fingers, or drawings to represent the collection in question. They count both parts to arrive at the whole, or they count and separate one part from the whole and count what remains to find the unknown part.

When children are ready to use counting strategies, they use the number sequence to count on. *Counting on* and other counting strategies, such as *counting up to* and *counting back from* are good strategies. Children will need many experiences with direct modeling and counting, however, before they have strong understanding of the *part/whole* relationships of even simple math facts such as 3 + 3 = 6.

Later, these very basic relationships will be important when working with larger numbers. So, for example, if children know that they need 3 more if they have 3 but want 6, they will also know that they need 3 more if they have 23 but need 26, or that they will need 30 more if they have 30 and they need 60. A strong foundation in number relationships enables children to use number operations with understanding and efficiency.

Implications for Teaching

As we review the three chapters on number, we can see that the compelling questions for children—*How many? Who has more? Is it fair?*—grow in complexity. *Number sense* concerns the attribute of numerosity. Children make meaning for numbers as they build connections among the representations of a given number (e.g., ***, *three*, 3, Δ). In the chapter on counting, we looked at how the structure of our number system provides us with a way to quantify any given set. After children learn to count, their next task is to build number relationships. In this chapter on operations, the questions become a bit more complex—we want to know *How many now?* when sets change, *How many more or fewer?* when we compare sets, and figure out the unknown in a part/whole relationship by composing and decomposing sets.

Young children's lives are filled with situations and with beloved tales that pose mathematical problem situations. If we want them to understand how joining/separating, comparing sets, or composing/decomposing numbers makes sense, we must mathematize those stories. Just as counting is meaningful only if we are *counting something*, children need to be given many opportunities to experience that *every operation tells a story*.

Foster Children's Strategies for Problem Solving

As their understanding develops, the thinking children bring to the story situations gets more complex. We have seen how very young children can understand the relationship between sets *as more*, *less*, and *equal to* before they can order or use number words or numerals to specify *How many?* As number sense and rational counting develops, children's skill in manipulating numbers also increases. They become able to make sense of arithmetic problems involving larger quantities that are stripped of their stories; at the same time, they will see "word problems" as expressions of the mathematical problem situations that are all around us rather than trick questions.

However, at all stages, children need to be actively engaged in making sense of the problem situation and its number relationships. That means they need to call on their informal knowledge and be encouraged to develop and try out their own solution strategies. Skilled teachers like Ms. Green know that the best way to make this happen is to provide many opportunities for children to discuss and explain their methods with peers and with teachers. They also regularly pose problems like the Fairy Tale Party posters that call for many different possible answers.

Table 4.1 outlines the most common strategies children tend to come up with and use; it indicates how children tend to use *direct modeling strategies* first; that is, they use manipulatives or drawings to literally represent the situation and try out a solution. As their ability to generalize and abstract increases, they rely on more sophisticated *counting strategies*.

As the descriptions in Table 4.1 suggest, there is a close connection between counting skills and a conceptual understanding of number operations. As we saw in the chapter on number sense, encouraging children to use their natural ability to subitize supports them in counting on from a number they

"just know," so too, the stronger their visual number sense is, the easier it is for them to recognize and use the way numbers can be composed and decomposed into. The more fluently children can count forward and backward from any number, instead of having to start at one, the more comfortable they are with solving number operations problems.

Developing and using strategies, however, is an ongoing process. As the counting sequence and math facts become automatic, children don't need to do as much direct modeling for simple operations. It is also true, however, that

TABLE 4.1   Development of Strategies for Number Operations

Problem Situations	Questions to Be Answered	Examples of Children's Direct Modeling Strategies	Examples of Children's Counting Strategies
Change situations	*How many now?* (joining)	**Count All:** counts out first set, counts out second set, then counts all	**Count On:** counts on from first number while keeping track of counts
	How many now? (separating)	**Count All:** counts out first set, counts and separates second set, then counts what's left	**Count Back From:** counts back from first number while keeping track of counts
Comparison situations	*Which has more/ Which has fewer?*	**Match:** lines up two sets with one-to-one correspondence	**Order:** counts both sets and determines which set is more by which number comes later in the counting sequence
	How many more/ How many fewer?	**Count Difference:** matches two sets and counts the ones left unmatched	**Count Up to Larger Number:** counts up from smaller number to the larger number
Part/Whole situations	*How many in the whole?* (composing)	**Count All:** counts out both parts, then counts all	**Count On:** counts on from first number while keeping track of counts
	How many in one part? (decomposing)	**Count All:** counts out whole, counts out given part from the whole, then counts the remaining part	**Count Up to Whole:** counts up from given part to the whole

they may well need to use concrete models or make drawings to make sense as they mathematize one of those "math all around us" problem situations where the number relationships are not quite as obvious. If we expect and support children to move back and forth between counting and direct modeling strategies, we are providing them with flexibility to model operations in whatever way works best.

Understand Factors That Affect Difficulty

There are several factors that affect the level of difficulty in a problem situation.

- Of course, the size of the numbers makes a big difference. Children are first able to use more advanced strategies such as counting on with smaller numbers, for which they have a good understanding and can use their subitizing skills. When first constructing the relationships between numbers, it is especially important for children to have lots of experiences with smaller numbers. This provides a strong foundation as their number sense extends into higher numbers.

- So, too, the problem situations that we ask young children to model or "act out" need to have a fairly simple structure. Just as Ms. Green kept asking "How many now?" with the gingerbread story, it is important to keep reminding children of what the "unknown" is. In general, finding *the result of a change* is the easiest to model—as we saw, Ms. Green's students were able to model both joining ($3 + 4 = ?$) and separating ($7 - 4 = ?$) situations.

- Many kindergarteners will need extensive guidance in solving situations that involve an *unknown change* ($3 + ? = 7$ or $7 - ? = 3$) or an *unknown start* ($? + 4 = 7$ or $? - 4 = 3$). Furthermore, operations that don't involve a change but call for composing and decomposing can also be challenging. The *part/whole relationships* between numbers within one set are more difficult to "act out" or directly model than a story in which an action changes the numbers of a set. As we saw, the children in Ms. Green's classroom could make their individual posters for the Fairy Tale Party, but she had to play a very active role in guiding the discussion that helped them see that 10 could be composed many different ways.

- Language issues make comparison situations difficult. To start, any comparison can be expressed in more than one way: *8 is more than 6; 6 is less than 8*. Even as you read those two statements, you may have noticed that asking *How many more?* seems easier than *How many less or fewer?* In general, children seem to be more interested in statements about what is "more"—*bigger, longer, higher, more, most;* they tend to find it uncomfortable to think of themselves as associated with what is "less"—*smaller, lower, fewer, fewest, least*, and this reluctance seems to carry over into mathematics.

- For any mathematical problem situation, knowing the story that lies behind the number operations helps young children make sense, but it also can pose challenges—for children whose first language is not English as well as for those who have language development issues. Before "mathematizing" a great story like the *The Gingerbread Man*, make sure the children are comfortable with it. Ms. Green, for example, had used the story as an interactive read-aloud and revisited it several times. Because dramatizing stories was a familiar activity, the children had no trouble with the "mathematical" version; in fact, although there were different levels of language proficiency, everyone contributed to the rich conversations about how the number of characters changes and compares. Giving children an opportunity to use felt-board figures or manipulatives to tell the story on their own and to model the problem situation provides opportunities for them to revisit and explore the situation again and again.

Focus on Understanding, Not "Right" Answers

Children benefit when teachers expose them to a range of problem situations without prescribing strategies. Children need many opportunities to solve problems with concrete objects, draw pictures to show their thinking, explain, and discuss their solutions in order to develop strategies that are meaningful to them. While it may take more time than simply teaching children procedures for getting answers, supporting children to solve problems in ways that make sense to them lays a strong foundation, and children are able to build on what they have learned to tackle new and increasingly advanced problems.

TEACHER TALK
Marilyn, Pre-K Teacher

I was puzzled when Bea told me that the fox "added one away" when he ate the Gingerbread Man. I asked her to show me what she meant and she pulled the gingerbread felt board figure off the board, explaining she was adding it away. That started a whole conversation about the meaning of the words "adding" and "taking away" that was really helpful to many children.

Finding Great Math in Great Books

Many of the books we identified in the counting chapter can be used to support the close relationship between counting and number operations. In fact, they can be used to help children understand that number operations are an efficient way to count—as the quantity grows, it is much easier to count on than to count one-by-one. Here are some more books that can help build meaning for number operations:

- *One Is a Snail, Ten Is a Crab* by April Pulley Sayre is a delightful book that "counts by feet"—that is, by the different number of feet various creatures have. Kindergarteners can write and draw math riddles such as *2 spiders: How many feet? Or 1 dog and 1 chicken: How many feet?*

- *Over in the Meadow,* available in several beautifully illustrated editions, and Sandra Boynton's wonderfully zany *Hippos Go Berserk* can be used to reinforce simple counting up. However, older 5- and 6-year-olds might enjoy figuring out how the total number of mamas and babies, or hippos, increases as the book goes on. Encourage them to use manipulatives to model how the total grows as the numbers increase to become fairly large (39 hippos, for example). As each new group joins in, you will be able to observe which children count on, or the point at which a child goes back to counting all.

- To spark rich conversations about comparisons, there's no better book to start with than Tana Hoban's *More, Fewer, Less*. This wordless book is full of photographs that invite both visual comparison and counting. The photographs depict everyday objects such as shoes for sale, fruit at the market, black and white piano keys, and silverware in a tray. Encourage children to describe the comparisons they see in more than one way; for example, *There are more blue spoons than red spoons* and *There are fewer red spoons than blue spoons.*

- We talked about using Emily Jenkins's *Five Creatures* to generate sorting situations. Another way to look at the story is to think of the book as showing different ways to compose and decompose the number 5. You might have children draw a picture of all the creatures in their house, both pets and people. They can dictate how the number in their own household is composed such as, *"At my house, there are three people and one dog"* or *"We have two kids and two grown-ups."*

▶ Video Link

In the *Mouse Collections* video clip, two teachers use the book *Mouse Count* by Ellen Stoll Walsh to get children thinking about how a collection changes in quantity. One teacher leads an acting out game with the whole class of children, and the other teacher works with a small group of children to tell a number story using props. With their bodies or with concrete objects, children learn about the ideas of change and comparison. As you reflect on what the video indicates about number operations, here are a few questions to consider:

1. How can having children act out number operations stories help their conceptual understanding?

2. What are your thoughts about the way these teachers put the emphasis on helping children see *change* in terms of more or fewer/less rather than on having them count to find the exact total?

3. Several of the children in the video are English Language Learners; what evidence do you see that they understand the Big Ideas though they don't articulate them in words?

Chapter 5

PATTERN
Recognizing Repetition and Regularity

Big Ideas about Pattern

- Patterns are sequences (repeating or growing) governed by a rule; they exist both in the world and in mathematics.
- Identifying the rule of a pattern brings predictability and allows us to make generalizations.
- The same pattern can be found in many different forms.

Math Snapshot

For several days now, the same group of four children has gathered on the floor near the math center to make connecting cube "trains" during center time. Their aim has been to make long trains, seeing which trains reach closest to the classroom door. Today, however, Ms. Rosa notices that the children's attention has turned to the color of the cubes and the talk is about making "patterns." She overhears Daniel announce, "My train goes orange, blue, orange, blue, orange, blue, orange, blue—it's a pattern!" Alicia, who is carefully choosing cubes for her train, replies, "Mine's a pattern too." Josie and Leo seem curious about making patterns and start to break apart their longer trains with a new purpose in mind.

From the earliest age, young children innately look for patterns in their world. Bedtime comes after bath and a book every night. There are five school days, followed by two home days each week. The human brain is predisposed to pattern, to find similarities that bind seemingly unrelated information together in a whole. Without recognition of pattern, children would experience all events as discrete, separate and unrelated. Children crave regularity because it allows them to predict what comes next and make sense of their world. While the search for pattern underlies all of learning, it makes a particularly powerful contribution to our mathematical understanding.

Virtually all mathematics is based on pattern and structure. By **pattern**, we mean any predictable sequence found in physical and geometric situations as well as in numbers. Patterns exist in many forms: a *visual pattern* might be in a floor-tile design or a stained glass window; *auditory patterns* include musical rhythms, clocks ticking, or the sound of footsteps; *movement patterns* are found in dance and walking; *temporal patterns* include hours and minutes, the days of the week, or the seasons; and *numerical patterns* show up in an array of square numbers, the sequence of odd and even numbers, or the predictability of the base-10 system.

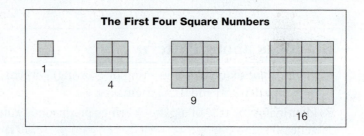

The First Four Square Numbers

By **structure**, we mean the ways in which various elements in a pattern are organized and related. For example, a simple repeating rhythm of *clap, stomp, clap, stomp, clap, stomp* has the same *structure* as odd and even numbers. Both patterns share the same alternating structure and can be represented by symbols such as AB. Describing the structure of a pattern requires us to look beyond its physical form to focus on underlying relationships, a highly mathematical approach to the world.

Pattern is less a topic of mathematics than a defining quality of mathematics itself. Mathematics "makes sense" because its patterns allow us to generalize our understanding from one situation to another. Children who expect mathematics to "make sense" *look* for patterns. For example, a child who looks for patterns soon realizes that counting words after 20 repeat the same sequence of a decade number word plus 1, 2, 3, 4, 5, 6, 7, 8, 9 (for example, 21, 22, 23, 24 . . . 31, 32, 33, 34 . . .). A child who does not recognize the regularity in the counting word sequence frequently gets mixed up and rarely is able to recognize or correct a mistake. Children need many opportunities to discover and talk about patterns in mathematics. These experiences help them form the attitude and confidence that mathematics *should* make sense—the crucial foundation all children need to become persistent and flexible problem solvers.

We have identified three Big Ideas that are key understandings about pattern in mathematics.

- With experience, young children get "tuned in" to patterns and deepen their understanding of the first Big Idea: *Patterns are sequences governed by a rule; they exist both in the world and in mathematics.* Teachers can build on children's natural tendency to find patterns everywhere in order to make children's knowledge more precise and mathematical.

- One way to think more precisely about how a pattern works is to identify its rule. The second Big Idea—*Identifying the rule of a pattern brings predictability and allows us to make generalizations*—helps children begin to extend their thinking from one situation to another.

- The third Big Idea is the most abstract: *The same pattern structure can be found in many different forms.* This understanding develops over time and enables children to see connections and think about relationships apart from their physical form.

These three Big Ideas can help guide you in determining what to highlight for children as they explore patterns. Since patterns are all around us, you will find that teaching opportunities arise naturally and frequently, and not just at "math" time.

Big Idea: Patterns Are Sequences Governed by a Rule; They Exist Both in the World and in Mathematics

Math Snapshot

Ms. Rosa joins the four children making trains and observes closely what they are doing. Daniel continues his alternating pattern of orange and blue until he runs out of orange cubes and announces that he is "done." Leo, wanting to imitate Daniel's pattern, is alternating colors but is not concerned which two colors he uses, switching at random intervals. So, his train starts with orange and blue, then alternates white and yellow, then green and brown. Josie, the youngest of the four, is selecting her cubes by color, making a train that is all red. Ms. Rosa notices that Alicia is building her train from the center out, adding the same colors to each end, resulting in a symmetrical design.

Do all these trains qualify as patterns? Clearly, Daniel's train of alternating colors has a predictable regularity—orange is always followed by blue; blue is always followed by orange. Leo's "chaining" method of alternating colors results in a train of many different colors. Is it a pattern? What about Josie's train of all red cubes?

When we think of patterns, what often comes to mind are sequences that repeat such as stripes on the American flag: *red, white, red, white, red, white. . . .* Indeed, repeating patterns are often the first kind of pattern that young children recognize and label as *patterns*. **Repeating patterns** are so named because they contain a segment that continuously repeats. We call this segment the **unit of repeat**. A unit of repeat can vary in length and level of complexity, but it is always the shortest string of elements that repeats. The unit of repeat can be thought about as the **rule** that governs a pattern. For Daniel's train, the unit of repeat is orange,

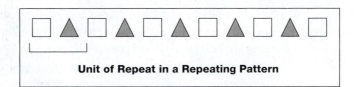

Unit of Repeat in a Repeating Pattern

blue. Leo's train does not have a consistent unit of repeat. Without that predictability, it cannot be considered a pattern, since it is not governed by a rule. Josie's red train may not appear to be a pattern at all, but it does indeed follow a rule of all red—its unit of repeat is simply red—and it is predictable. This kind of regularity is common in everyday life. Think of a sidewalk, a picket fence, or a ringing telephone. The unit of repeat is a single item—a concrete slab, a fence post, or a ringing sound.

A useful way, as an adult, to think deeply about how and why patterns are mathematical is to construct a pattern, perhaps with blue, red, and green connecting cubes as your unit of repeat. Continue the pattern for at least three repetitions, often referred to as *iterations* in mathematics, and then number each connecting cube in the sequence. Do you notice any relationship between the numbers and the color pattern? What color will be in the 27th position? What color will be in the 301st position? It's the structure of the pattern that underlies it—whether we see it in a series of colors or a series of numbers—that allows us to make these amazing predictions with such accuracy.

Young children like those in Ms. Rosa's class are likely to spontaneously explore repetition and regularity given materials such as beads or blocks or musical instruments. However, like Leo, most will not apply a rule *consistently*; that is, the unit of repeat is not constant throughout the sequence. This is an example of how receptive understanding precedes productive understanding; he probably can recognize patterns, but maintaining one over a long structure of connecting cubes is beyond him right now. Children detect patterns in their world and know when the rule has been violated—think of the children's protests when your daily schedule deviates from the usual routine—long before they are able to create their own stable patterns.

Since Ms. Rosa notices that many of her children are receptive to repeating patterns, she looks for opportunities to build on that. One day, when reading aloud *Brown Bear, Brown Bear, What Do You See?* by Bill Martin Jr. and Eric Carle, the children chime in with the words. Acting surprised, Ms. Rosa asks how the children know what comes next. Marcos explains, "It repeats the same every time." Ms. Rosa extends his thinking by saying, "Yes, you're right. The words have a *pattern*." Ms. Rosa is not surprised when later that week, Marcos announces that the song *This Old Man* has a pattern, too.

Children need diverse experiences with repeating patterns, and they can also work with growing patterns. **Growing patterns** increase or decrease by a constant amount. In this case, it is not a segment or string of elements that repeats, but a quantitative change that repeats. The most basic growing pattern is found in our counting system: 1, 2, 3, 4, 5. . . . The rule of this growing pattern is plus-one; the regular quantitative increase by one is what brings predictability to this sequence. For young children, growing patterns are best understood concretely, using geometric models. For example, if you stack connecting cubes in towers and line up the towers in order of size, children will see the resulting stair-step structure of a plus-one growing pattern.

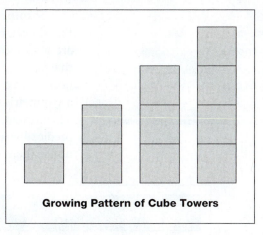

Growing Pattern of Cube Towers

Ms. Rosa knows that many cumulative tales in children's books illustrate the growing pattern of increasing by one or decreasing by one. She selects one of the class favorites, *The Napping House* by Audrey Wood, to explore with the children. Using picture cards of the characters, Ms. Rosa helps the children represent how on each page, one more character piles onto the bed. As the growing pattern is revealed, the children get excited because they can figure out "what comes next."

While repeating and growing patterns are most often represented in a linear form, many real-world patterns are nonlinear. Nonlinear patterns are common in nature, and in art or designs such as those found on clothing and wallpaper. **Concentric patterns** have circles or rings that grow from a common center. Examples include ripples in still water after you throw a pebble or a nautilus shell.

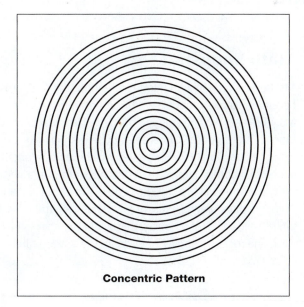

Concentric Pattern

Symmetrical patterns have segments that repeat, but instead of being in a line, they are organized as mirror images of one another; that is, they extend outward in different directions from a line or a point. Butterfly wings are a symmetrical visual pattern, as are snowflakes. These examples are patterns because they are predictable and rule-governed, and children notice them in their everyday lives.

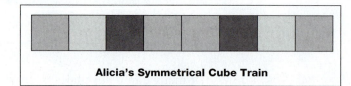

Alicia's Symmetrical Cube Train

One way to informally assess children's receptive understanding of pattern is to go on a **Pattern Walk**. This activity is a good way to *mathematize* the patterns that children might notice every day such as the railings on the stairs, the tiles in the hallway, or the numbers on classroom doors. Helping children "tune in" to the patterns all around reinforces the Big Idea that patterns exist both in the world and in mathematics.

Big Idea: Identifying the Rule of a Pattern Brings Predictability and Allows Us to Make Generalizations

Math Snapshot

Ms. Rosa asks the children to tell her about their patterns. Daniel right away repeats his announcement that his pattern is "orange, blue, orange, blue, orange, blue." Ms. Rosa asks why he stopped building. Daniel explains that he ran out of orange blocks, "so I stopped 'cause it has to be orange next. See? It's always blue, then orange." Ms. Rosa asks Leo to describe his pattern and he shrugs his shoulders. She suggests that they "read" the pattern together. In a sing-songy voice to exaggerate the alternating pattern, Ms. Rosa points to each cube and leads Leo to chant, "orange, blue, orange, blue, orange, blue . . ." then "white, yellow, white, yellow, white, yellow . . ." She notices that when Leo chimes in, he tilts his head back and forth and rocks his body slightly as they chant together.

Daniel knows repeating patterns have rules, and he's defined the rule of his pattern. He understands that to use a different color than orange would interrupt the regularity of the sequence and make it impossible to predict what might come next. Leo, on the other hand, is just beginning to explore repeating patterns. When Ms. Rosa helps him "read" his pre-pattern sequence, she is giving him the chance to *feel* the regularity of the alternating colors visually, verbally, and kinesthetically. This chanting and rocking is a means to help Leo recognize the repeating nature of a pattern. Ms. Rosa provides a developmentally appropriate degree of challenge by inviting Leo to join her, as he is ready to do so.

Young children like Leo benefit from opportunities to **copy**, or duplicate, well established patterned sequences. Ms. Rosa plans an activity for Leo and other interested children called **Jewelry Shop**. She strings beads in different AB color patterns to create models for children to copy. She is careful to show at least three complete *iterations*, or repetitions, of the AB unit to establish the repeating nature of the pattern. Ms. Rosa asks the children to help the jewelry shop get ready for customers by making more necklaces just like the ones she shows them. This activity allows children to explore repeating patterns within a structure that indicates what comes next.

During center time, Ms. Rosa visits with the children at the Jewelry Shop. She observes to see who can copy an AB pattern and whether anyone extends or creates their own. Ms. Rosa plans to challenge children who are ready to try to copy the ABB and AABB patterned necklaces she has prepared. She is pleased to see how many children choose to work at the Jewelry Shop. Leo's explicit interest in patterning, and Ms. Rosa's involvement and intervention, encourage other children to join in creating patterned necklaces. This is useful mathematics in a play-based context.

However, just because a child can copy a pattern does not mean that the child can identify its rule. The next week, Ms. Rosa creates an activity to help focus children on a pattern's rule, by "breaking it." Using pattern-block shape stamps, Ms. Rosa prepares linear, repeating shape patterns on sentence strip paper. Again, she presents three or more iterations of the pattern but intentionally omits one or two elements for children to **complete** in an activity called **What's Missing?** Ms. Rosa gives children a bin of pattern blocks and asks them to "fix" the pattern by figuring out what is missing. Ms. Rosa sits with a small group and asks children questions such as *How do you know what's missing?* and *Are you sure?* She wants to focus children on the regularity and structure of each pattern to build understanding of the Big Idea that patterns are sequences governed by rules.

What's Missing?

Children who are never asked to identify the rule of patterns will have difficulty extending patterns, especially as they become more complex. Knowing the rule of the pattern allows one to predict what comes next. Ms. Rosa uses an ongoing math activity at rug time to give children plenty of opportunities to **extend** a pattern. In **Movement Patterns**, the teacher presents a pattern using body movements as the repeating element, such as a pattern with the unit of repeat (reach up, reach down, hands on hips). The children are invited to join in as soon as they recognize the pattern. Once most children have joined in, the teacher says, *Freeze!* and asks the children to name, or predict, what comes next in the sequence—*How would this pattern keep going?* In this way, children begin to identify the rule and extend it. After talking about how the pattern "works," the teacher leads the movement pattern again. **Movement Patterns** provide scaffolding for children to extend patterns with support from the teacher and peers. And, the multiple modalities of the activity put the math into the hands, eyes, ears, and feet of the children. The goal is generalization—recognizing how patterns can grow or be extended.

Big Idea: The Same Pattern Structure Can Be Found in Many Different Forms

Math Snapshot

Ms. Rosa invites a small group of children, including Daniel and Alicia, over to the rug. She reminds them about the activity with movement patterns. She tells them that she has a question for them: "Can you make a cube train to match my movement pattern?" She begins with a clap, tap, clap, tap, clap, tap . . . pattern. Most of the children look puzzled at first, but Daniel lights up and says, "That's like my orange and blue pattern!" Ms. Rosa asks Daniel to tell more, and he explains, "The clap can be blue and the tap can be orange. It goes one and then the other." He starts making a train to demonstrate. Meanwhile, Alicia starts a train, alternating white and green. Ms. Rosa asks her to share, and Alicia says, "My pattern goes white for clap and green for tap." She points to the white and green cubes and slowly says, "Clap, tap, clap, tap, clap, tap . . ."

Are these preschoolers doing "algebra"? Having one thing stand for another is the beginning of algebraic representation. Such naming helps children recognize relationships between patterns that have different physical embodiments. The ability to consider the common structure, rather than physical appearances, is highly abstract.

So, yes, these children are thinking algebraically! But, as you've seen, it is the result of many opportunities to work with patterns in various forms—color, shape, movement—and many opportunities to describe the rule of a pattern by naming the smallest unit that repeats.

Ms. Rosa plans an activity called **People Patterns** to give the children a chance to analyze and describe patterns. Using half the class as the audience and half as participants, she arranges the children in a pattern: stand, stand, sit; stand, stand, sit; stand, stand, sit. . . . Ms. Rosa asks children in the audience, who can see the pattern more clearly from a distance, to **describe** the pattern. She asks questions such as *How could we name this pattern? What is its rule?* Once the children decide that this pattern is named "Stand, Stand, Sit," Ms. Rosa invites individual children to join the sequence in the next position.

As children from the audience join the people pattern, Ms. Rosa gathers informal assessment information about which children are able to identify the rule and extend it. She notices that some children seem to discern the order of the elements in the pattern without necessarily recognizing the rule. To extend a pattern, they simply copy the given sequence. This works when the pattern model ends neatly at the end of the unit of repeat (i.e., AABAAB . . .). However children who do not see the underlying structure of the pattern have trouble extending a sequence that ends in the middle of the unit of repeat. For example, Josie goes back to the first element of the sequence (i.e., AABAABAA<u>A</u>) rather than extend it. This kind of information helps Ms. Rosa know who needs more help to establish the unit of repeat, and who is ready to think about relationships between different representations of the same pattern.

Recognizing the same pattern structure in different forms (for example, visual and movement patterns) is a crucial step in using patterns to make generalizations. At least by kindergarten, children can **translate**, or transfer, a pattern to other forms. The earliest translation is from visual or auditory form into spoken words. When Ms. Rosa and Leo "read" his connecting cube train, saying "orange, blue, orange, blue," they are effectively translating the pattern. Eventually, children can explore translating between different media such as Ms. Rosa did with movement and color patterns (for example, "clap for each blue, tap for each orange").

Another activity to try is called **Pattern Match**. In this activity, children are given pattern models in one medium, such as pattern-block shape pattern strips, and asked to find matching patterns in another medium, such as colored bead necklaces. Questions such as *How are these patterns the same?* help children to go beyond the materials making up the pattern to see the fundamental mathematical structure involved.

We do movement patterns as part of our Morning Meeting. Each child has a turn to help the class "record" the pattern of the day. At first, they use invented symbols such as X | X | X | ... for clap, jump, clap, jump, clap, jump.... Then once a child uses letters or numbers, she explores representing patterns using variables such as AB.

Ultimately, children can translate two or more like patterns to a common format by using some form of symbolism to represent the structure of the pattern. Whether children use the standard symbols such as AB or their own invented symbols, this is another foundation of algebraic representation.

The search for pattern is a habit of mind we want to encourage in all young mathematicians, right from the start. Children must see all mathematics as a search for patterns, structure, and relationships, as a process of making sense of physical, geometric, and eventually numerical, situations. Only then will they have the necessary foundation for algebraic thinking.

Implications for Teaching

With patterns, as in all mathematical areas, there is a need for teachers to both plan specific activities and capitalize on children's math-related play. Also, teachers need to elicit and guide mathematical discussions in both settings.

The work we do with children in early childhood classrooms mostly concerns simple repeating patterns. Familiar repetitive sequences such as color or shape patterns are accessible to young children and model the regularity and structure inherent in patterns. While this represents but a small portion of pattern concepts, it lays the foundation for children's understanding to expand to growing patterns and numerical patterns in later years.

Developmental Trajectory for Patterns

As we looked at the activities in Ms. Rosa's room, we have seen ways in which pattern activities can build on and support each other. Table 5.1 indicates the kind of activities that help children develop an understanding of the Big Ideas, organized by children's typical developmental progression.

Visual patterns are the easiest for children to work with because they present multiple *iterations*, or repetitions, of the pattern's unit of repeat. In contrast, rhythmic or movement patterns, for example, are fleeting—iterations of the unit of repeat do not last over time. Still, children should be exposed to a variety of patterns in differing modes and orientations, lest they develop the misconception that patterns are embodied only in linear sequences of colors and shapes. Exploring different forms of pattern—auditory, temporal, visual, movement—provides children with different opportunities from which to abstract the concept of what makes a pattern: regularity and structure.

When we model patterns for children, it is important to *present at least three iterations of the unit of repeat*. It is necessary to reveal the structure of the pattern

TABLE 5.1 Activities for Exploring Patterns

Activity Type	Description of Child's Competency	Example Instructional Task	Teacher Talk	Big Idea
Recognize	Detects regularity, applies the word *pattern* to simple repeating sequences	*Pattern Walk; Who Is Napping?*	*Do you see a pattern here? Do you notice anything that repeats?*	Patterns are sequences governed by a rule; they exist both in the world and in mathematics.
Copy	Duplicates simple patterns alongside a model pattern	*Jewelry Shop*	*Can you copy this pattern? Does yours follow the same rule?*	
Complete	Fills in missing element of pattern	*What's Missing?*	*How can you fix this pattern? How do you know what's missing?*	Identifying the rule of a pattern brings predictability and allows one to make generalizations.
Extend	Continues a pattern	*Movement Patterns*	*What comes next? How would this pattern keep going?*	
Describe	Identifies the rule of a pattern by naming the smallest unit that repeats	*People Patterns*	*How could we name this pattern? What is its rule?*	
Translate	Uses new media to construct pattern with the same structure as model pattern	*Pattern Match*	*Can you make this pattern another way? How are they the same?*	The same pattern structure can be found in many different forms.

to children before asking them about it. Likewise, continue to verbalize the pattern past the last iteration to reinforce the idea that the pattern could continue indefinitely.

Consider Materials and Level of Pattern Complexity

Early patterning activities should include concrete materials that children can manipulate. This makes it easy for children to try to extend patterns and make changes to self-correct. Your choice of materials for patterning should take into consideration many of the same factors discussed in the chapter on Sets. **Color** is often the most salient visual attribute for children, so materials such as connecting cubes that vary only by color may be a good first choice.

Shape and **size** are other visual attributes to repeat in patterns. Patterns such as square, circle, circle, square, circle, circle, square, circle, circle; or big rock, little rock, big rock, little rock, big rock, little rock focus children on attributes other than color. It is important, at least at first, to remove color as an attribute when working on shape or size patterns. For example, hexagon, triangle, hexagon, triangle, hexagon, triangle is a shape pattern, but if all the hexagons are yellow and all the triangles are green, then it is also a color pattern. So, provide all same-color shapes (for example, hexagons *and* triangles are natural wood color) or materials such as multicolored rocks that vary by distinct sizes to focus children on repeating attributes other than color.

Later on, one way to increase the level of pattern complexity is to use materials with multiple attributes. For example, a pattern constructed with attribute blocks might have the unit of repeat: little, red circle; big, yellow circle. Even more advanced, the following shape pattern, red <u>circle</u>, blue <u>triangle</u>, blue <u>circle</u>, yellow <u>triangle</u>, blue <u>circle</u>, red <u>triangle</u>, requires children to isolate the attribute of shape while negating the attribute of color. Clearly, higher-order thinking such as this builds on many experiences with both creating and naming sets by attributes, and many experiences with patterns.

Within all pattern forms, the level of complexity can be adjusted by varying the length of the unit of repeat (AB vs. AABB) and by varying the number of elements in the unit of repeat (AB vs. ABC). Other more complex pattern structures insert subpatterns into the unit of repeat (for example, ACDBCDACDBCD . . .) or introduce growing patterns into a sequence (for example, ABAABAAABAAAAB . . .). It is often children themselves who stumble on these more complex pattern structures in their spontaneous play. For example, Marco in Ms. Rosa's class built a patterned fence in the block corner using the unit blocks in different spatial orientations. He described his ABAC pattern as "post, fence, post, gate; post, fence, post, gate; post, fence, post, gate . . .".

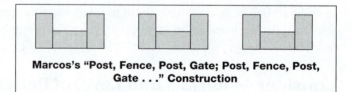

Marcos's "Post, Fence, Post, Gate; Post, Fence, Post, Gate . . ." Construction

Be On the Lookout for Child-Made Patterns

Table 5.1 outlines a general pathway of understanding that most children take when working with patterns that are modeled, at least in part, for them. The sample instructional tasks are activities that a teacher can intentionally plan to scaffold children's understanding of pattern in a sequential way.

However, a parallel pathway exists for the patterns that children *themselves* **create**. As we've seen in the Math Snapshots, children in Ms. Rosa's classroom spontaneously created patterns and prepattern sequences during play. Young children are inclined to spontaneously create alternating patterns or symmetrical patterns, as those seem to be naturally pleasing to them. However, just because a child creates a pattern does not mean that she is aware of the pattern's rule; she could be creating it without realizing it. For example, a child could create a patterned sequence on a pegboard by taking pegs from alternating buckets of red and blue pegs and placing them in a row. Although the child is repeating an action sequence, she may not be aware of the visual color pattern she is creating. As children gain more experience with the Big Ideas of patterns, the patterns they create will reflect their increasing understanding that patterns are rule-governed and that a rule can be described with words. In fact, the more children are encouraged to explain how their pattern "works," the more likely they are to identify the unit of repeat.

Describe and Discuss Patterns to Build Understanding

Describing patterns is difficult for young children. Their implicit, informal knowledge about patterns takes many experiences, scaffolded by a teacher, to become more formal, mathematical knowledge. Language is the tool by which this happens.

When children are exploring patterns, ask them to explain how a pattern "works." Children will likely respond in one of two ways: a chanting response or a unit-of-repeat response. For example, given the color pattern RGYYRGYYRGYY . . . , a child may say, "It goes red, green, yellow, yellow, red, green, yellow, yellow. . . ." Or, a child may talk about the unit of repeat, as in "It is one red, one green, and two yellows." A unit-of-repeat response is evidence that the child is aware of the pattern's rule. The child who gives a chanting response needs more opportunities to generate a rule that defines the pattern. You can ask follow-up questions to help children focus on regularity and repetition, such as, *What do you notice about this pattern? What part repeats? How could we name this pattern? What is its rule?*

Once children "tune in" to patterns all around them, you will likely hear them *over*-apply the word *pattern*. Young children label many events as "patterns" even when the unit of repeat has not been well established. For example, in Ms. Rosa's classroom, Amelia announces that the snack table has a pattern because "it goes girl, boy, girl." Ms. Rosa helps Amelia extend her thinking by asking her, *How does this pattern continue? What comes next? Can you think of another pattern like this one?* With a classroom of pattern detectives, you will have many opportunities to talk about patterns in meaningful contexts throughout the school day.

Use the Classroom Environment to Explore Patterns

The opportunity for young children to explore patterns can be integrated right into the routines and structures of your classroom. Common routines such as reviewing your daily schedule or constructing a weekly calendar help children identify patterns in time. In another example, the names on Ms. Rosa's job chart rotate in a predictable pattern so that her students are quick to figure out how many turns until they will be Line Leader again. These routines build children's understanding when we offer feedback that helps them see the underlying mathematical concepts. We must actively engage in discussing the mathematics with children in order to build understanding.

You can set up your classroom to promote children's explorations of pattern.
Observe what children do with the materials and prompts you've provided, be ready
to highlight the math as it emerges within
play, and ask questions such as *How do you
know?* and *Are you sure?* Think about how
to make patterns an everyday part of your
classroom:

- Children often create patterns in their artwork. Provide materials with multiple colors and textures. Stamps and stencils, which are easy to repeat, lend
  themselves to repeating patterns.

- Symmetry and repeating patterns often emerge in children's block buildings.
  Provide photos of real buildings as models of patterns for children to copy.

- Most songs and finger plays incorporate patterns. Point out and help children describe the patterns. Then, create new patterns as you sing new versions of familiar
  songs. For example, instead of, "The Wheels on the Bus Go 'Round and 'Round,"
  create a song for fall, "The Leaves on the Trees Float Down and Down."

- A basket of percussion instruments such as shakers, tambourines, rhythm
  sticks, and triangles invites children to create simple rhythms. Have two or
  three children compose a pattern together.

- Outside, children may physically feel patterns such as a swing going back
  and forth or a ball bouncing up and down. They may also find patterns in
  nature, such as flower petals or birdcalls. You can help children describe
  what they notice.

- Patterns can be found in many children's books. Whether the pattern is
  in the language or the illustrations, books provide a wonderful context for
  pattern exploration. See suggestions below.

Finding Great Math in Great Books

Many well-loved children's books incorporate pattern because it supports young children's literacy development. Children use language and picture patterns to "read"
predictable books. They often use or extend language patterns from books in their
own story dictation. Patterns support children to predict what will happen next in a
story. These literacy skills overlap with a mathematical understanding of pattern, and
you will want to, at times, shift your read-aloud objectives to focus on the math. The
following books make pattern explicit. They are good choices when you want to plan
an intentional discussion about patterns and how they work.

- *Lots and Lots of Zebra Stripes: Patterns in Nature* by Stephen R. Swinburne. This book is full of large, colorful photographs of patterns found in nature such as a spiral spider web, markings on a caterpillar, and stripes on a watermelon rind. The simple text points out the structure of the patterns: *Some patterns are straight lines* (trees in a woods). *Some patterns are curved lines* (rainbow). It helps children develop the Big Idea that patterns exist both in the world and in mathematics.
- *I Went Walking* by Sue Williams and *Brown Bear, Brown Bear, What Do You See?* by Bill Martin Jr. Both of these books have simple, repeating words that children quickly learn. Asking children to identify the words that repeat helps them "mathematize" the patterns they hear.
- *Rooster's Off to See the World* by Eric Carle. The simple cumulative tale tells of rooster's journey to see the world. As he walks along, animals join him in groups that increase by one animal each time (i.e., two cats, three frogs, four turtles, and five fish). This growing pattern is represented in the margins with animal icons, making the stair-step structure of the pattern evident to children.
- *The Napping House* by Audrey Wood. Another cumulative tale in which characters pile on a bed, one by one, to nap. The plus-one growing pattern is easy for children to describe because the illustrations distinctly show the growing, linear sequence and foreshadow "what comes next."
- *Pattern Bugs* by Trudy Harris. This book highlights the Big Idea that the same pattern structure can be found in different forms. The rhythmic sounds of the poems, the details of the insects, and the decorative borders on each page share the same pattern structure (AB, ABB, etc.) Children love using this book for a pattern hunt!

▶ Video Link

Children explore a simple growing pattern in the video clip called *Who Is Napping?* As you watch, think about the following questions:

1. How does the teacher *mathematize* the story in the book *The Napping House* by Audrey Wood?

2. What do children notice about the shape of the growing pattern? How is this particular pattern connected to our number system?

3. Growing patterns are often overlooked in early childhood classrooms. What evidence do you see that these young children can recognize and think about this kind of pattern?

Chapter 6

MEASUREMENT
Making Fair Comparisons

Math Snapshot

The sand table has been one of the most popular free play choices in Ms. Marty's mixed-age preschool classroom. She's stocked it with different sizes of scoopers (coffee, laundry) and measuring cups and containers. She notices that all morning Addie, Ben, and Sora have been involved in an intense discussion about which one of the clear containers in the sand table is the biggest. She realizes this is one of those "math all around us" moments she can use to develop the children's thinking about measurement.

Questions about *What's the biggest?* get raised again and again in early childhood settings. As adults we are quick to see that solving this particular dispute calls for a systematic *comparison* of the containers; we also recognize that before we can make the comparison, we must determine *what kind of bigger* is involved. Do we mean which container is taller? Wider? Or, is it a question of which one holds most—that is, which has the largest capacity? Each of these attributes calls for a somewhat different way of carrying out the comparison. If we want to know just how much bigger the "biggest" one is, we'll get out a measuring tool: a ruler, a tape measure, or a measuring cup. Then we'll announce the results by quantifying the difference: "This jar is six-and-a-half inches tall and that one is six-and-three-quarters inches, just a little bit taller." Alternatively, we might avoid numbers altogether and settle for a direct comparison, lining the containers up tallest to shortest, or widest to narrowest, or from that which holds the most sand to the one that holds the least. In each of these situations, we are engaging in **measurement**.

Interestingly, as adults we often don't recognize that any time we are dealing with measurement, we actually rely on a great deal of mathematical thinking. We are so used to the chain of reasoning involved that we overlook how complex a process it actually is for young children. For example, as natural as it is for us to express measurements in numbers of **standard units** such as inches or pounds, young children often aren't ready for the kind of abstract thinking that gives such units meaning. Instead, their conviction that one thing is "bigger" or "biggest" is quite likely to depend on perception—if it looks bigger, it must be bigger.

Technically speaking, *measurement* is any process that produces a quantitative description of an attribute, such as length, circumference, weight, temperature, volume, or number. Measurement is an essentially mathematical procedure that we apply in many different contexts, such as space and time (think of miles and months) and in many different ways, such as measuring the height of a desk (30 inches) versus the capacity of a bucket (6 gallons). In our daily life, we often wish to know how many beats per measure, how many more minutes until preschool is over, how hot it is today, or whether I am taller than my friend. In all these circumstances, we use some kind of *comparison* process to measure or to answer the question *How much?* or *How many?* For the purposes of this chapter, we will limit our discussion to the measurement of **length** (think height, width) and **capacity** (think size of containers). Attributes like length and capacity are more readily apparent and meaningful to young children than less visible ideas like temperature and time.

We have identified three Big Ideas that young children need repeated opportunities to experience in order to understand what it means to measure.

- Young children who have a chance to notice that *many different attributes can be measured, even when measuring a single object*, are more likely to think about, notice, or point out which **attribute** is being considered whenever a discussion is about size or number.

- When children have many opportunities to make and discuss comparisons, they become more competent with the procedural requirements of measurement, since *all measurement involves a "fair" comparison*. Making direct comparisons in the preschool classroom is critical preparation for later, more sophisticated indirect measurement activities and builds the conviction that to be accurate, measurement must be fair.

- Repeated, meaningful experiences with comparison will lead children quite naturally to understand that *quantifying a measurement helps us describe and compare more precisely*, as they find it deeply satisfying to use their growing sense of numerosity to say exactly "how much bigger."

The central challenge in helping very young children understand measurement concepts is to slow down our expectations for the learning process. What seems like a simple set of procedural requirements to most adults masks a series of concepts, each of which adds a new level of complexity to children's thinking. By ensuring that young children have multiple opportunities to explore these ideas, you can help them build a meaningful understanding of measurement that will support their later use of more conventional and sophisticated measurement techniques.

Big Idea: Many Different Attributes Can Be Measured, Even when Measuring a Single Object

Math Snapshot

Ms. Marty uses a simple observation to start the children thinking. "Children, I notice that each of you thinks a different one of the containers is biggest. Let's have each of you tell me what you think and why." Addie is quick to hold up a wide, squat peanut butter jar and declare, "This is biggest because it's so fat across." She motions with her hands over the jar and then brings them in close above the other two. "No, Addie," Ben says, "It's bigger to be taller, like this one," and he points to a narrow-necked ketchup bottle. Sora is a little hesitant but says, "When I pour from this one to the other one, it spills out so I think the first one gets the most fuller." Ms. Marty smiles and says, "I can see that each of you is thinking about what makes the jar you chose biggest. But did you notice that each of you is talking about a different kind of big?"

As Ms. Marty makes her way over to the sand table, she isn't planning to suggest a procedure to come up with a "right" answer. Instead, she is thinking about how to help the children realize that before figuring out the answer, they need to work on their questions. As the children's responses so clearly indicate, they all have a different idea as to what *bigger* means. In mathematical terms, they are thinking of different *attributes*, each of which has a measurable size.

The way that Ben talks about *height* as bigger while Addie focuses on *width* is quite typical of young children. Height and width are two different ways to measure **length**, each representing a different dimension. Length attributes like these are easy to visually compare, so children tend to notice them naturally as they think about the world. Height in particular is very salient to children, perhaps because the floor provides a standard baseline for many objects that can be easily compared—sometimes no adjustment is necessary to "line things up." But in certain contexts, such as with the containers, other length attributes, like width, will eventually capture children's attention. It takes many experiences and conversations before children really

TEACHER TALK
Gloria, Pre-K Teacher

It's surprising how often a child about to turn 5 is convinced that once he has his birthday he will be "bigger" in every way—including taller, stronger, and more able to do things. I remember my son came in the day he turned 5 and asked if it really was his birthday—he was sure he would be able to reach the sink to brush his teeth without using the stepstool!

understand that there are different kinds of "bigger," and that in order to make good comparisons of length, it is important to be measuring the same *dimension* of each object.

Sora's statement about how the sand spills out when she pours from one container to another concerns the attribute of **capacity**, that is, the amount of a given substance that a container holds. While capacity is usually not visually comparable the way that length is, it becomes very salient for young children at the sand or water table, where it is fun to watch something overflow. Eventually, children conclude that if the contents of the peanut butter jar spill over when poured into the ketchup bottle, the peanut butter jar must be bigger in some important way. The fact that it is sometimes difficult to make good visual comparisons of capacity means that something might look bigger but hold less—a discovery that always takes young children by surprise and can eventually (with teachers' guidance!) prompt them to think carefully about attributes and measurement processes.

With different types of size—like capacity and circumference—and different dimensions of objects—like width and height—playing such a big part in measurement activities, it's easy to see how complex measurement is. There is much for young children to think about, discuss, and discover before they will be ready for more conventional, adult-like measurement activities that involve the use of measuring tools and abstract ideas like ounces or inches.

Big Idea: All Measurement Involves a "Fair" Comparison

Math Snapshot

Ms. Marty's comment about different kinds of "big" captures the children's interest. Soon Ben, Addie, and Sora are busily lining up containers in the sand table from shortest to tallest. Then they reorganize the containers from "fattest" to "skinniest." They can't agree on a way to compare them since it's hard to judge how big around each container is. Ben turns to Ms. Marty and declares, "It's too hard to see the fattest!" She nods and says, "You were able to see the *tallest* really easily, weren't you? But now you want to know which one is the *longest all around*—that is pretty tricky!" She adds, "Watch this and see if it gives you any ideas." She picks up an 8-ounce margarine container and holds it against the opening of a plastic coffee cup; Addie claps her hands in delight as she sees that even though the margarine container is somewhat shorter, its mouth is clearly wider. "See, Ben!" she crows, picking up the peanut butter jar and the ketchup bottle, "This one is bigger this way!" Ben shrugs and says,

(continued)

"It's just the hole that is bigger; taller is still the real biggest," and wanders off to another activity.

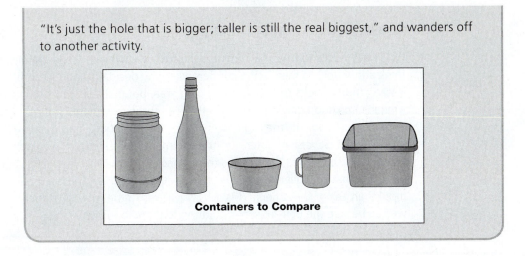

Containers to Compare

As adults, we might smile at Ben's conviction that taller is always biggest as typical of the way children aren't really logical. From a developmental perspective, however, his belief does make sense—it's a reflection of the way young children are quite concrete and literal. Sensibly, they believe what they can see: thus the children in Ms. Marty's classroom are able to compare the containers' heights simply by lining them up next to each other and looking. In mathematical terms, they are measuring by making a *direct comparison* and then ordering them from shortest to tallest. Ms. Marty's suggestion to compare the circumference of the containers— what Ms. Marty describes as the "length all around"—by placing their openings against each other is another example of direct comparison.

It is also no surprise that Ben is reluctant to accept that "his" ketchup bottle does not have the widest circumference. All of us who work with young children know that they are incredibly attuned to issues of what's fair, and that *winning*—being the *biggest/best*—is also tremendously important. Precisely because they are still struggling with the idea that there can be different ways of being *bigger* (or best), they need many experiences that will give them different ways to compare, and to do so in a way that is demonstrably *fair*. Very likely, Ben felt that comparing the small opening of the ketchup bottle to the opening of the peanut butter jar was not "fair" because the ketchup bottle is wider at its base than at its top.

As adults, our many experiences of *biggest* or *fairness* tend to override the way young children see these questions. It is obvious to us that biggest is a **relative** term: that is, what is "bigger" in one dimension can change when the same set of objects is measured using a different attribute. We grown-ups have no trouble understanding that the tallest jar might also be the most narrow. However, young children are convinced only that these differences can co-exist after many experiences. They need the *comparisons and the conversations*—using visual, tactile, and verbal inputs and interactions to help persuade them that the conclusion they have reached is right—and fair.

Ms. Marty is a wonderful example of a truly "intentional teacher." She knows that a successful lesson goes beyond simply selecting an activity. She realizes that she needs to think about the details of the materials she uses, as well as the kinds of questions and prompts. In this case, she recognizes that while belts normally go "around," it will be easy for the children to **directly compare** the lengths of the belts when one belt is laid on top of another. She has also deliberately chosen only black or dark brown ones so that the children will focus on dimensions of length, rather than color. Controlling the attributes of the belts helps promote the kinds of comparisons she believes the children need to make to move their learning about measurement forward.

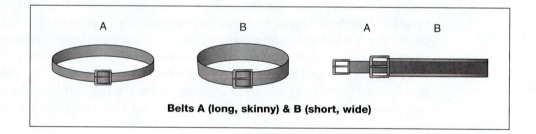

Belts A (long, skinny) & B (short, wide)

Ms. Marty is delighted to see the spurt of activity that happens with the belts in the housekeeping area. As the children begin to buckle the belts, they physically experience how length and circumference are related. She overhears several conversations about which "hole" makes a belt a good fit for each child, moving the conversation further toward ideas of circumference. Now, Ms. Marty believes that children are ready to compare the widths of the containers from the sand table using paper "belts."

Math Snapshot

Ms. Marty sets out strips of adding machine tape of various lengths at the math center along with the containers from the sand table. She invites the children to trim the pieces to measure the length all around the containers—like a belt! After making a number of these belts, Kaya and Ben come over to Ms. Marty, filled with excitement, saying, "We can use the belts to tell which containers are 'fat' and which ones are 'skinny'!" Kaya measures out a length to go around the upper edge of a yogurt container. Ms. Marty helps her cut it to just the right length to complete the circle. Ben uses another strip to circle the upper rim of a wide-mouthed margarine container, explaining, "It's got to be fair; I put the belt in the same place." Once both belts "fit," they undo them and lay the paper strips side by side. Kaya slides hers so that it extends past Ben's strip. Ben corrects her, saying "It's only fair if they start at the same place and just like the same!" Kaya accepts this idea, and they carefully align both paper strips to the edge of the table.

As we have seen, many of the children's explorations involve *direct comparisons,* in which two objects are physically arranged so that the key attributes of each are fairly aligned. However, comparing the paper strips rather than the cylindrical containers themselves adds an important new complexity: now the children are exploring *indirect comparisons.* As is true in many real-life situations, it is difficult to directly compare some attributes; instead we use a tool like the adding machine strips (or a tape measure!) to **represent**, or stand in for, the size of the attribute being measured. Through their experience with the belts, the children learned they can turn a circumference into a length, which is easier to measure. In this case, **direct comparison** of circumferences doesn't happen between the two containers; instead it happens between the two *representations* of their circumferences, the two paper strips. Because this kind of comparison utilizes representations to stand in for the attributes to be compared, we call this an *indirect comparison.*

Indirect comparisons can have another advantage—in real life, direct comparisons are sometimes not possible or not practical. While it's usually best to try on clothes in person (a direct comparison), indirect comparison means we can compare the inseam of a pair of well-fitting pants to a new pair of pants to determine whether or not they will need to be hemmed (an indirect comparison). There are situations that lend themselves to indirect measurement in the lives of young children, as well. When schools have big rolls of colored paper they use to cover bulletin boards, these can provide a rich opportunity for meaningful indirect measurement activities.

In one kindergarten classroom we know of, the teacher wanted to use red paper to cover a large table for the class Valentine's Day party. By asking the children how they could be sure how much paper they needed to cut, she helped the children come up with the idea of using a piece of string, cut to the length of the table. By taking the string with them to the giant rolls of paper, they had a representation of the table's length. Children were highly satisfied to see the paper fit the table beautifully. Many experiences coming up with and using such portable representations of size are needed before young children will be ready to understand the purpose of a ruler or tape measure.

Big Idea: Quantifying a Measurement Helps Us Describe and Compare More Precisely

Math Snapshot

Kaya is proud to show Addie that the paper "belt" for the margarine container is longer than the one for the peanut butter jar. Addie concedes that "hers" is not the longest all around, but tells Kaya, "Yours isn't very long, maybe only 1 or 2 longer." Kaya disagrees and says, "No this one is lots longer. It's 10 long." Ms. Marty quickly intervenes to steer the disagreement toward productive learning. She grabs two baskets of connecting cubes from the shelf, and she asks, "Do you think these could help us count how long all around each one is?" Kaya and Addie use the cubes to make a train as long as each paper strip and then count to see how many cubes each one has. Kaya finds hers is 8 cubes and Addie finds that hers is "almost" 6 cubes long.

Counting to compare works beautifully when comparing two sets of things. The children in Ms. Marty's classroom understand that if there are 12 chocolate cupcakes and 6 vanilla cupcakes, there are more chocolate cupcakes! The idea that counting can be used to compare not only two sets, but also the length of two objects is an important revelation for young children. It is this nonobvious application of counting to the comparison of size attributes that creates a crucial measurement concept: the **unit**.

Inches, pounds, and ounces are not things, but ideas. Conventional units such as these subdivide a single size attribute in order to make it countable. In effect, these units turn attributes such as length, weight, or volume, into sets—sets of units of uniform size. By bringing out the connecting cubes, Ms. Marty has supplied units that are already the same size—measuring the length of the paper strips with rocks of different sizes or the children's hands would not work quite as well.

As adults, we have a much simpler way to figure out how much longer one thing is than another—we use a ruler or tape measure and quickly calculate the difference in inches or centimeters. But once again, Ms. Marty knows that it is more important to let the children think and problem-solve than to hand them an answer. Furthermore, she knows that the concept of an inch or a centimeter is a convention that we've internalized long ago but that does not yet mean much to young children.

By bringing numbers into her measurement activities, Ms. Marty has implicitly endorsed the idea of precision. The reason for *unitizing* size attributes is to create greater precision in our comparisons, so that we can say *how much* bigger. For Kaya and Addie it isn't enough to know which paper strip is longer; they feel they need a way to tell *exactly* how much longer. Essentially, unitizing and counting add information to our descriptions of size attributes by mathematizing comparison processes. With such precise, quantifiable descriptions, it becomes possible to convey size information reliably, so that we can purchase just enough cloth or cut a board to the right length. Applying number to measurement allows us to conduct the advanced calculations that are the foundations of architecture and engineering.

Unquestionably, it is difficult for adults to recall how we as children first made sense of measurement. We are so conditioned to think in terms of *inches/feet*, *ounces/pounds/tons*, *yards/meters*, *quarts/liters*, you name it. It's no wonder we think that measurement is all about conventional units. But as we have seen, there are at least three important concepts children need opportunities to understand.

The Big Idea that *many different attributes can be measured* emphasizes the importance of understanding the nature of the attribute to be measured and the need to focus on it, to the exclusion of the object's other attributes. Only then can a comparison be made, and *all measurement involves a "fair" comparison*. While we are quite aware of important measurement procedures, such as the need to use units of uniform size, we may have lost sight of the fact that we do this so that measurement will be fair. Adults tend to underestimate the important shifts in thinking that occur when children see that indirect comparisons mean that measurement can be accomplished using representations, or tools. And finally, we must remember how big a revelation it is that we can unitize attributes to allow us to "count" size, *quantifying measurements to compare and describe more precisely*.

Young children need many experiences that will help them to see each of these things for themselves. They need to make direct comparisons and ensure their fairness. They need opportunities to solve real measurement problems, so they can see the usefulness of measurement tools. They need experiences using connecting cubes, or links, or some other uniformly-sized manipulative, to see how units work and how precisely they can describe size. These are the experiences that will make the eventual use of rulers and inches make sense.

 ## Implications for Teaching

The intersection between language development and mathematical thinking is a central issue in terms of understanding measurement. In fact, as we have seen in exploring Big Ideas of sets, number, and patterns *expressing relationships between things is much more complex* than naming concrete items or actions. Just as "three" does not name a single thing, but only different sets of three things, there is no such thing as *big* without comparison to something that is *small*.

Both ideas—number and size—are inherently relational; their meaning hinges on relationships between things. Because measurement is a process of description, the way we describe attributes throughout the classroom is particularly important. *Longer* is both distinct from *wider* and more precise than *bigger*. *Heavier* is a very different idea from *taller*. Being aware of how you use comparative adjectives like these is a good way to begin thinking about measurement in your early childhood classroom, but there are other pieces to consider as well. In this section, we provide a sense of how ideas about measurement develop, and discuss different aspects of teaching that can make your classroom measurement-rich!

Important Questions That Build Understanding about Measurement

As we looked at the activities in Ms. Marty's room, we saw ways in which the Big Ideas about different *attributes* of size, direct and indirect *comparison*, ensuring *fairness* in measurement, and understanding of *units* build on and support each other. One useful way to think about children's developing theories of measurement is as a series of important questions to be asked. Each of the Big Ideas suggests a new and important set of understandings that truly shifts children's thinking. By focusing on these, we help children build the intellectual structures that will eventually support a meaningful understanding of conventional measurement. Table 6.1 presents each Big Idea, pairing it with the kind of question children should be thinking about as they engage each one. We have also included some of the teaching points that come up as each Big Idea is explored, and suggested some ways these ideas might be prompted by activities in your classroom.

While this table lays out a general learning path, it is important to recognize that children make their own way, sometimes leaping to a complex understanding for one exploration or retreating to a beginning level later. It takes many experiences to fully establish understanding. For example, Ben is not particularly concerned about which container in the sand table is biggest; for him it is a question of which is tallest. However, comparing attributes of dinosaurs is quite a different matter. He has put a great deal of time and mental energy into comparing them in multiple ways. He knows that T. Rex was not as *long* from head to tail as many plant-eating sauropods and that he didn't *weigh* as much; still, T. Rex was much *more fierce*, with teeth and claws that were both *longer* and *sharper*; furthermore he could run and destroy his prey *faster*!

Encourage Children to Measure for Authentic Purposes

Ben's ability to understand fine distinctions in measurements involving dinosaurs and the

TABLE 6.1 Using Important Questions to Teach about the Big Ideas

Big Idea/Important Question	Teaching Points	Classroom Experiences
• Many different attributes can be measured, even when measuring a single object. *What kind of bigger is it?*	• We can measure lots of things, like how much it will hold OR how tall it is. • There are even different kinds of length measurements: height (taller/shorter) is a different dimension than width (thicker/thinner).	• Provide children with examples of rich, descriptive language for size, such as "thinner" and "longer." • Help children identify dimensions, using both language and gesture.
• All measurement involves a "fair" comparison. *How can we compare?*	• Measurements are about relative size—not just "long" but "longer than. . . ." • When it's hard to directly compare, we can use a representation of the size, or a tool (indirect comparison).	• Have children find things in the room that are the length of their handspan. • Make a paper "foot" for each child and do the same activity—the paper foot allows them to compare their foot to things posted on the wall, for example.
• All measurement involves a "fair" comparison. *How can we make it fair?*	• There are rules for measuring, like using a baseline when comparing lengths. • To compare two objects, we need to measure the same attribute, such as circumference.	• Ask children to define their own rules for a "fair" comparison. For example, when measuring the length of your foot, do you measure with your shoe on or off? • Use language that is specific to the attribute in consideration, for example, *wider, heavier, 7 cubes tall.*
• Quantifying a measurement helps us describe and compare more precisely. *How much bigger is it?*	• We can use numbers to make comparisons more precise. • We have to use equal-size units if we want to create an accurate measurement.	• Go on a "measurement hunt," finding things that are 4, 6, and 8 links long and writing/drawing them on a clipboard. • Measure the same object with connecting cubes and then with links—compare the outcome.

way the children got involved exploring circumference with belts illustrate another important principle about bringing mathematics to life in early childhood classrooms: the *more authentic the measurement problem-situation is, the more deeply children are likely to be engaged* in thinking, exploring, and extending their understanding.

As we have seen in Ms. Marty's classroom, virtually every area of an early childhood classroom, from the sand table, to housekeeping, to the math center, offers authentic situations for exploring measurement. Intentional teachers are always on the alert for such situations. Some might be handled with a spontaneous "teachable moment." However, it is equally important to take the time to reflect and plan a coherent sequence of activities to develop understanding, as Ms. Marty did with the containers in the sand table and the belts.

Be on the Lookout for Measurable Moments!

When you are watching for them, there will be many opportunities to informally mathematize the concepts and language of measurement. You might note how books in a stack have different dimensions or how drinking straws are shaped like the pillar blocks, but are both longer and thinner. You could also establish an ongoing *Bigger This Way, Bigger That Way* display in your classroom. Encourage children to look for examples of items that are bigger in different ways. For example, a child might choose a large snake and a giraffe from a collection of plastic zoo animals. Use a digital photo or a drawing of the two and have the child dictate a label such as "The snake is longer. The giraffe is taller." At group time, invite the child to share his discovery before posting it on the display.

Finding Great Math in Great Books

Given young children's preoccupation with getting bigger and growing up, it is not surprising that many outstanding works of children's literature can be linked to measurement. Here are a few of the Early Math Collaborative's favorites.

- *The Growing Story* by Ruth Krauss is a wonderful classic celebration of how a little boy sees the growth in farm animals and in plants over the course of several seasons but keeps wondering if he himself is growing. Her *Carrot Seed* also makes a natural link with a science exploration of how plants change in size and appearance as they grow.
- *Tall* and *Where's My Teddy* are two of Jez Alborough's delightful picture books that offer very child-friendly explorations of how what's big and what's little depends on who or what you are comparing.
- *Tikki Tikki Tembo* by Arlene Mosel is another classic with a built-in measurement problem situation. A Chinese mother learns the dangers of giving her older son a long name. The story is a great way to launch investigations of the length of names; at the same time, children find chanting Tikki Tikki Tembo's full name irresistible fun for the tongue that builds phonemic awareness.
- *Next to an Ant* by Mara Rockliff uses illustrations and a very simple repetitive text to make the point that while next to an ant, a berry is big, next to a berry, a shoe is big (and so on). Writing your own classroom version of this story is a rich way to mix mathematics and literacy. This book is also available in Spanish.
- *Actual Size* and *Prehistoric Actual Size* by Steve Jenkins will have young scientists poring over them. How else could they compare the actual size of a gorilla's hand to their own or find something as long (and sharp) as a shark or a dinosaur's tooth?

▶ Video Link

There are two video clips of measurement activities in preschool classrooms, one about length and one about capacity. In both activities, children are given compelling reasons to make direct comparisons and share their findings.

As you watch the video clip *Just Right for Me*, here are some points to reflect on:

1. How does the teacher make use of gesture and language to define the attribute of length?

2. This classroom has been reading different versions of *Goldilocks and the Three Bears*. How does the idea of "just right" connect with a familiar tale and connect to measurement concepts?

3. What evidence do you see that the children are deepening their understanding of the Big Idea that all measurement involves a "fair comparison"?

When viewing the video clip *Which Holds More?*, here are some points to reflect on:

4. Consider the importance of having authentic reasons to measure. How are the two different questions in the two classrooms relevant to the children?

5. Capacity is a difficult idea to describe with language. What evidence of receptive understanding do you notice?

6. In what ways do these teachers help children use measurement to prove (or disprove) their perceptual judgments?

Chapter 7

DATA ANALYSIS

Asking Questions and Finding Answers

Big Ideas about Data Analysis

- The purpose of collecting data is to answer questions when the answers are not immediately obvious.
- Data must be represented in order to be interpreted, and how data are gathered and organized depends on the question.
- It is useful to compare parts of the data and to draw conclusions about the data as a whole.

Math Snapshot

The first snows came this year in early November. It's now just after Thanksgiving and the Lost and Found box in Ms. Daniels's junior kindergarten is already filled to overflowing. At drop-off and pick-up times, many parents are expressing their frustration at having to replace all the newly purchased cold weather wear. Hats, scarves, single gloves and mittens are missing, as well as a few pairs of snow pants and extra sweaters.

Ms. Daniels knows scolding or constantly reminding the children to keep track of their things is unlikely to work. She feels this is an important problem for the classroom community to work on together. At the same time, she recognizes that this is a natural opportunity for mathematizing, since any "big mess" of items lends itself to sorting and quantifying—key activities for an inventory form of data analysis. She plans to open the investigation at the Monday morning meeting by asking the children to help her "sort out" this problem, knowing she should be able to build on the work the children have been doing all fall around sorting and patterns to push their thinking into issues of data.

For many early childhood teachers, the words "data analysis" are associated with detailed charts and graphs, computers, and sophisticated ways of analyzing numbers, and so seem like a very strange thing to be talking about with young children. Other teachers know that data analysis can be very simple, like making a list of items and writing how many you have of each in parentheses, or creating and talking about a bar graph whose bars are higher for snowy than rainy days in the month of January.

Whether the process involves specialized statistical software or markers and chart paper, what remains the same is that data analysis gathers information in a quantitative way (*how many?*), and then organizes it in some way that makes comparison and generalization possible. That is, we create a new picture or story about the information, one that emphasizes some kind of measurement—such as cardinal amount—and that shows or tells the information more efficiently, creating a simpler but more powerful set of ideas. Through the process of analyzing the data, we learn something new.

Ms. Daniels's idea is a good one. Knowing what is in the box is an important first step to coming up with a plan to address the problem. Clearly gloves and mittens are going to account for the biggest number of losses. But scarves and hats are likely to take up more space in the box—to say nothing of bulky sweaters, snow pants, and whatever else might be in there. In order to understand the problem well and to come up with ideas for preventing its reoccurrence, Ms. Daniels and her students will have to study the contents of the Lost and Found bin in a few different ways, creating a useful teaching opportunity focused on data analysis.

To help you think about the most important data analysis concepts for young children, we have identified three Big Ideas that can help guide your classroom explorations:

- The most important thing young children can learn about data analysis is *why we do it.* When children see that the *purpose of collecting data is to answer questions when the answers are not immediately obvious,* they understand why data analysis is useful. That motivates children to try it and to try to understand how it works.

- With scaffolding and thoughtful guidance, young children can follow the steps involved in a simple data analysis process. When they have several different experiences under their belt, meant to answer different types of questions, they begin to see that *data must be represented in order to be interpreted, and how data are gathered and organized depends on the question.* This Big Idea about data analysis comes only with experience, but when it does come, it makes children feel powerful and prepared to take action to understand their world.

- Finally, the Big Ideas in data analysis get back around to its purpose, once again. Children need the help of a thoughtful adult to see that *it is useful to compare parts of the data and to draw conclusions about the data as a whole.* This crucial final step, in which we use the data to learn something new, makes the entire process of analyzing data make sense to young children.

If you let these three Big Ideas guide your use of data analysis activities in your classroom, the children you work with will learn that quantitative information is something they can do something about. They will feel empowered to reorganize it to create answers to questions and to discover new questions that they did not have before. They will know that a chart or graph is meant to tell them something useful, and will want to figure out what that is. By including thoughtful and meaningful experiences of data analysis, your classroom can help prepare children to be creators and users of data for a lifetime.

Big Idea: The Purpose of Collecting Data Is to Answer Questions When the Answers Are Not Immediately Obvious

Math Snapshot

On Monday morning, Ms. Daniels puts the overflowing Lost and Found box in the center of the circle. She says, "I've been hearing from you and your parents that many of you have lost your outdoor things. This is a real problem for everyone. But look at the Lost and Found—it's full! What can you tell me about why you haven't been looking in it?"

Children are quick to offer explanations, many of them pointing out that the box is so packed it is hard to see what is in it.

Ms. Daniels asks children to think for a moment about what their classroom community might do to help solve this problem and then turn and talk to a partner about their ideas. She then calls on individuals to share their thinking.

"Tomi and I think we need a bigger box," says Fawn.

"Patti and me had a different idea—we think we need more boxes so the same kind of stuff can go in one," another child chimes in.

"We think the biggest box has to be for gloves and mittens," declares one boy. "NO! Remember, PJ—we said just mittens in one!" the partner interjects.

Ms. Daniels is recording the children's observations and suggestions on chart paper. She lets the children know she will leave the Lost and Found box out during free choice time and that they will come back and talk more just after lunch. She reminds them that missing their things is a big problem, so they need to think hard about what is the best way to start finding solutions. She adds that she knows what good thinkers they are and is excited to see what kinds of answers they will come up with.

When dealing with young children we often overlook the fact that *for authentic problem solving to take place, there must be an authentic problem—one whose solution is not obvious or predetermined.* As adults, we have so much more experience and such a detailed conceptual framework that we can find it hard to break down problems into discrete steps that will help young children construct their own understanding.

We can find it equally challenging to let children freely explore—to let them propose solutions an adult would quickly reject, to try things out, and then to revise and rework both the questions and the answers that immediately pop into their minds. In many ways, opening problem solving up to young children is not terribly efficient. However, taking the slower step-by-step approach is much more effective in the long run. As they struggle through trial and error, with teacher guidance, the children will be developing habits of mind that characterize lifelong learners.

In effect, that means that the questions, surveys, and data collection activities we do in preschool or in kindergarten have to be held to the same standard as those posed by professional survey experts. If the data and the results are obvious and predictable, collecting and analyzing is mechanical, with no real problem solving or thinking involved. Counting and writing down how many of each color crayon we have to determine which one we have the most of is not that interesting when they are already sorted into the red cup, the blue cup, and the green cup and it is obvious that the greens outnumber everything else. In the end, we want the young child and the brilliant computer programmer to struggle with the same initial question—*What kind of data should I collect so that I will have answers to questions to which I don't know the answers or that I don't yet realize are important?*

In terms of the Lost and Found Box, that might mean asking *What kinds of winter wear get lost most often? Do the data suggest any reasons why this might be so?* as well as *What kind of winter wear takes the most room in our boxes?*

Big Idea: Data Must Be Represented in Order to Be Interpreted, and How Data Are Gathered and Organized Depends on the Question

Math Snapshot

During free time, Ms. Daniels doesn't interfere when Jack and Toni dump out the Lost and Found box, so they can look for Jack's Bears hat and Toni's hand-me-down sweater. But she does ask if they want to start sorting into piles of related items. Soon, Tanya, Fawn, Kennie, and Joy join in.

By the end of free choice time, there is one fairly large, bulky heap of snow pants and another about the same size of sweaters and sweatshirts. The bunch of scarves looks bigger than the collection of single gloves and mittens—though there are clearly more hand-wear items. The pile of hats and caps is about the same size as the pile of scarves.

By the time the class gathers around for the afternoon meeting, some of the sorters have reclaimed lost items. Still, the piles on the rug are huge. Ms. Daniels agrees to find cardboard boxes or plastic tubs for each pile of related items. At pick-up and drop-off time in the next few days, parents express their delight about how much easier the new system makes it to check for lost items.

At the Wednesday morning meeting, Ms. Daniels notes the progress that has been made in emptying the Lost and Found; but she points out that none of the boxes are empty yet. "Using more boxes does make it easier to find things. But we still have a big problem—there are still lots of things being lost. What ideas do you have about helping us discover what *kinds* of items are getting lost most often? Once we know that, we can think about ways to help everyone keep track of that item." After some lively discussion, they appoint teams of two or three investigators to count how many items are in each of the five boxes and to report the results on Thursday.

Ms. Daniels knows that the children may quite easily get confused with what they have or haven't counted, especially when there are a lot of items to count. So she gives some sets of investigators a collection of connecting cubes of a given color. She suggests that the teams work together; one person will take an item out of the box and the other will add another connecting cube to the stack. As we saw in the measurement chapter, children who are not yet rationally counting can use the cube towers to *directly compare* how many items of each category are in the Lost and Found box.

Ms. Daniels also intentionally steers Fawn and Joy to take responsibility for the largest collection of items, the mittens and gloves. She knows they can rationally count beyond 20 by ones and enjoy chanting skip-counting by tens and fives. The girls do have several stacks of yellow connecting cubes available but she knows building a tower for this collection is likely to be very cumbersome.

She has been modeling and doing "think-alouds" about how tally marks can be a useful way to represent groups of five, when she is doing housekeeping tasks such as sorting lunch money or figuring out how many supplies she needs. Ms. Daniels sees the Lost and Found project as a way to get her soon-to-be kindergarteners to start thinking about how items might be grouped, for example into sets of five.

Math Snapshot

Ms. Daniels carefully observes as Fawn and Joy start their investigation. She can see they are a little overwhelmed by the large number of items they have to count. To make the task easier, they break them into two piles. Fawn can count gloves and Joy will do mittens. But once the piles are set, Ms. Daniels comments, "That was a good idea to sort this huge pile into two. Are there any others ways we could break down each of your piles?"

(continued)

Joy starts to make separate piles of mittens; at first she breaks the big pile into smaller units. Ms. Daniels is careful to keep her voice neutral as she comments, "Joy, I see that these two piles have five lost mittens and these two each have four."

Joy moves one mitten from one group of four and adds it to the other and declares, "Look I can do three groups of five, but there has to be one more smaller pile, because there aren't any more mittens."

She turns to Ms. Daniels and says, "The cube tower would be too big, I think. Can we just write down how many?"

She smiles and asks, "I'm not quite sure what you mean—are you going to write out the numbers one by one?"

Joy shakes her head. "No, I want to do the tallies like you do, that's much faster." She quickly points to the first pile and puts down four slashes and then one across. She does the same for piles two and three. She hesitates for a moment as she gets to the last pile and then slowly makes three tally marks. Joy stares at the paper for a while. Then she quietly counts 5, 10, 15 pointing to the first three tally groups. "This one has only three," she says with a frown. She hesitates for a moment and then counts on "So 16, 17, 18! There are 18 mittens."

Tally Marks

As each group finalizes their results, Ms. Daniels helps them transfer their findings to a bar graph that she has set up on large-scale graph paper. Using the grid lines already in place, she has written numerals at columns 5, 10, 15, and so on up to 30. While she knows that the youngest children will depend on the visual difference between the length of the bars, having the numbers will help support the older children's number sense. On the floor underneath, Ms. Daniels has lined up the bins with their lost items. The bins are in the same order as the rows on the bar graph. She is hoping that this will allow the children to compare how full the different bins are and see how this is different from which bins have more individual items, which is what will be represented by the bar graph.

As you can tell from this description, Ms. Daniels has thought quite deeply and carefully about how to help the children represent the data. In an inventory, this transition from the "raw data" to a new way of organizing it that emphasizes quantity is the really tricky part. Often, it is difficult for children to follow the thinking, and see the relationship between the "real things" and the resulting data display. The more connections that can be made between objects and ideas that are truly familiar to the children and the data representation that is created, the more likely children are to see the chart or graph as meaningful rather than "magical."

To preserve these kinds of connections, Ms. Daniels has the children report what kind of clothing they counted and the total number based on their cube towers. She writes the name of each category, and then with the class, counts from left to right along the row to show how many clothing items in each category (for example, "one, two, three" for the snow pants). She marks that spot and fills in the whole length of the bar with a marker. This deliberate process, involving the children in the thinking at each step, increases their opportunities to understand how each of the bars is related, in a very real way, to a set of items.

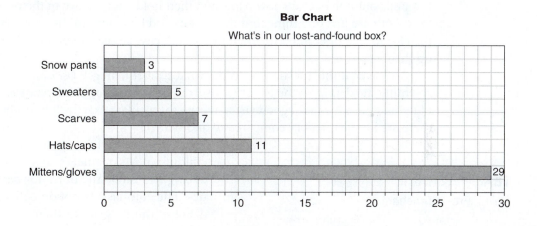

Bar Chart

What's in our lost-and-found box?

The children all have comments to make as the whole group reviews the data. Several point out that while there are only three snow pants and five sweaters, these two bins are completely filled while there is plenty of room in the bin with seven scarves. But what strikes everyone is how the bar showing the total of 29 mittens and gloves sticks out much farther than the bars for all the other categories. Ms. Daniels carefully facilitates the conversation to give the children ample opportunity to wrestle with the different ideas of quantity and size.

As the children look at the final bar graph, Ms. Daniels reminds them that different pairs of investigators used different methods to come up with the number of items in the different bins. It was easy for the two youngest children in the group to count the snow pants—since there were just three of them. Those who did the caps and hats found using the connecting cubes helpful. However, they decided to use red connecting cubes for the caps and purple for the hats to show that more hats were in the bin. Finally she holds up Fawn and Joy's tally sheets and comments, "Even though you used different ways to do your counting, we are using a bar graph *to represent* the results. *Represent* means the particular way we use to show our data. This bar graph is something grown-up mathematicians often use!"

Ms. Daniels knows that there are two questions of interest; that is, are we interested in which category has the most items, or which takes up the most space in the bin? To support children's attempts to answer these questions, Ms. Daniels has intentionally varied the way the data get represented by presenting them simultaneously in the bins (emphasizing space) and through the bar graph (emphasizing quantity). By contrasting these two forms of representation simultaneously, she is building the children's foundational understanding of the second Big Idea of Data: *Data must be represented in order to be interpreted, and how data are gathered and organized depends on the question.*

The level to which each bin is filled is a kind of informal **object graph**, that is, a graph made with real things. Everyone can see from the bins that bulky items like snow pants and sweaters take *more room* in the Lost and Found. Even so, Ms. Daniels encourages several children to comment on why these bins are so full. Kat pulls out one pair of snow pants and then holds out a glove in the other hand. "See, both are just one thing, but there's lots and lots more to the snow pants than the glove." The bins, lined up in a row, make it easy to see which objects are taking up the most room.

However, if the question concerns what type of item *gets lost most often*, representing the data with the bar graph is a much clearer way to *compare quantities* of items. It also creates a good visual means to calculate exactly *"how many more"* there are in one category compared to another.

The kind of rich exploration that the children in Ms. Daniels's room are experiencing should be the norm for data activities. The emphasis is not on collecting the data but thinking about them. Comments about what the results show are likely to lead to a new round of questions and conversations. In fact, the rule of thumb should be that at least twice as much time is spent analyzing data results as was devoted to collecting it.

With continuous experience, even young children begin to realize that collecting data isn't a popularity contest. Even when a survey looks at preferences (favorite color, food, book), a good discussion will celebrate the fact that there was a diversity of opinions—that we can each have a good reason for preferring what we do—and we can get new ideas by listening to another perspective.

Big Idea: It Is Useful to Compare Parts of the Data and to Draw Conclusions about the Data as a Whole

Math Snapshot

Ms. Daniels raises a new question about the Lost and Found bin at the class meeting the following week. "All that work we did last week sorting and thinking about the Lost and Found means that lots of the things you lost have been found again. That's great. However, on Friday, I ended up putting a few new items in the hand-wear and in the head-wear bin. So I'm wondering if we can start thinking about this problem—what can we do to help us all stop losing things?"

She pulls out the bar chart the children made last week, and says "We know that more gloves and mittens get lost than anything else. If we can figure out why, maybe we can come up with a way to make it happen less. Let's do a turn and talk. Turn around knee to knee and face each other. Then discuss why you think so many more gloves and mittens got lost than other things."

The children consider a variety of factors.

"There aren't that many snow pants because not everyone wears them. Besides you always tell us at dismissal to put on our snow pants."

"There's only one of a hat or a scarf but two of mittens and gloves."

"It's easy for one glove to fall out of your pocket."

"Mittens and gloves are small so you don't know when they are lost."

Ms. Daniels summarizes the discussion. "Many of you are commenting on how mittens and gloves come in pairs so that there are more of them that come to school every day. You also said that you can lose just one. You also are saying that because the hand-wear is smaller, it's easier for one to fall out of a pocket or get misplaced. Does anyone have any ideas about ways we could do a better job of keeping track of them?"

Kat says that her mom is always telling her to pay more attention and to always put things away in the same place so she won't lose them. Joy wonders if there should be a list for everyone to check off that they have both their gloves. Several children show the mitten clips their parents have provided to help keep their gloves attached to their coat. "Those look cool," Franky says. "Can you send a message about them home so my mom can get me some?"

The way Ms. Daniels refocused the discussion of the Lost and Found data is a good
example of how collecting and analyzing
data around authentic questions often will
naturally extend into new analysis and new
problems. In this case, once they had established that items of hand-wear were lost
most often, it made sense to turn the class's
thoughts to why that might be so and what
might be done.

In fact, raising everyone's awareness of
an issue by collecting data often has a positive effect all by itself. Certainly it did in this
case. The class voted to create a new weekly
job that called for counting up the number
of items in the Lost and Found by category.
The results were kept on a chart that the group revisited periodically to see how
they were doing. Ms. Daniels and the parents were delighted to see the number
of lost items definitely was on the decrease.

Implications for Teaching

Many early childhood teachers see doing surveys and making graphs as an easy
and fun way to do math. Very often, conducting surveys and representing the results as a graph becomes a way of measuring preferences: children chart favorite
colors, flavors of ice cream, or type of apple. However, young children are strongly
inclined to assume "more" means "better"; setting up surveys or graphs as votes
tends to make the children think in terms of winners and losers. No matter what
their real preference is, some children will go with what seems to be the majority
opinion. That tends to short circuit the rich mathematical thinking that data invite.

However, as we saw in the investigation of the Lost and Found box in
Ms. Daniels's room, collecting data about a real-life issue in order to use it to answer a question and help solve a problem is much more powerful. Surveys and
inventories done as *fact-finding* can actively give ownership of a problem situation
and its solution to the children. At the same time, using such situations engages
children in higher-order thinking and puts the focus on the *discussion* and *analysis*
of the results rather than just the collection of data.

Design Data Investigations for Deeper Understanding

As we have said several times, collecting data is not an end in itself. There
should always be a reason—a question that can be answered only if we have

more information. In effect, data are an important contribution to a problem-solving process. Thus, the first step is to define the focus. In early childhood classrooms, many investigations emerge naturally from interests, conditions, or issues. In Ms. Daniels's class, parents' concerns and the overflowing Lost and Found box made it clear that there was a problem. In such cases, it can be tempting for the adults to mandate that each child is to look through the box and claim their belongings and the rest will be donated. However, Ms. Daniels recognized that while it might be less *efficient*, in the long run it

TEACHER TALK
Jen, Pre-K Teacher

The children began to appreciate how important it was to think about exactly how we phrased our questions when we started to do a survey of family pets. Several children had both a cat and a dog and were upset that they might get to count only one. A few others felt left out because they didn't have any pets. So we all agreed that we would set up the survey so that we would find out how many families had pets and how many didn't. Then we would do a second graph showing how many pets were dogs, cats, hamsters, or whatever. That got tricky too: Jorge declared there were 15 fish in his father's aquarium and Anya's hamster just had had babies again. In the end, everyone agreed that the fish and the hamsters should be counted as one type per household, since the actual number kept changing, and Jorge and Anya insisted that we put a note at the bottom of the chart explaining that.

would be more *effective* to involve the children in the problem-solving process. The way that she invited them to begin by looking purposefully at what was in the Lost and Found box engaged the children in mathematical thinking, talking, and learning.

Once the problem or question has been identified, and you have figured out what kind of data to collect, the method to be used to collect it emerges naturally. An **inventory**, such as the Lost and Found investigation, will begin with *sorting* items into categories, and then *counting* how many in each category and recording the total. However, once all the counting is done, it is often helpful to **represent** the results in *a graph or chart* that compiles the data in a way that will help answer the original question. In the Lost and Found investigation, the question about what kinds of things were filling the Lost and Found box to overflowing had two parts. One concern was space: they needed to understand what kinds of items were taking up the most room in the bin. The other concern was about number of items: they thought that if they knew which kinds of items were lost most frequently, they could think about some ways to prevent the problem. Ms. Daniels used the filled bins to represent the data in one way and the bar graph to represent it in another as the group analyzed the data.

It's also true, however, that data do not always involve a manageable concrete collection of items that can be sorted and inventoried. Rather, the data are sometimes collected by conducting a **survey**, in which responses to a set

I used to think that doing surveys was basically a way to get the kids counting in a way that would be more fun for them. We didn't really look at the results except to verify the totals for each column and then say which had more or less. It did feel a little mechanical. But over the years, I started asking the children what thoughts they had about why the data turned out the way it did. I am always amazed how much they notice and the questions they ask!

Now it seems I don't have to come up with so many new ideas—if we have a good discussion about a set of data, the children will have more questions they want to investigate. As part of our Celebrating Families Project, we gathered data on who had relatives who lived nearby or far away (we defined that as having to drive more than two hours or fly). Several children got interested in exactly where different families lived—we ended up getting a map of North America and found if we included uncles, aunts, and grandparents, our classroom had relatives from Alaska to southern Mexico.

of questions are compiled and analyzed. The two major types of survey are:

- **Fact-finding surveys**, which involve objective data about objects or ways of doing things. Many classrooms, for example, will develop a chart showing the different ways children get to school, be it by walking, biking, car, or bus. Or there might be a survey of what kind of pets children have at home.

- **Preference surveys** or polls, in which people select among two or more options to indicate their personal preference. In some cases, like deciding the name of the classroom pet, having the majority rule is a practical solution, and the preference survey functions like a vote. Children need to understand that having another name chosen than the one they wanted doesn't mean there is anything wrong with the one they preferred. Once children establish the habit of mind that data call for analysis, surveys that examine preferences are less likely to be seen as a contest. Rather, as children start to talk about a survey question, for example, what makes a season of the year their favorite, they learn to appreciate that preferring one thing over another is not a question of right or wrong, good or bad. Rather it is evidence of the wonderful fact that each of us has a unique blend of sameness and difference with others.

Dynamic Classrooms Invite Data Analysis

Opportunities to use data analysis to mathematize your early childhood classroom can be found in every corner. For example:

- Do inventories of classroom materials such as Ms. Daniels did with the Lost and Found box. You might have children investigate questions such as, *How many creature toys do we have: How many are dolls? How many stuffed animals?* Or you might involve children in some kind of inventory of the books that are in the classroom library. Issues of space, fairness, and the rotation of materials can all provide reasons that will keep such investigations meaningful.

- Make attendance routines more dynamic by regularly exploring data about the children and their lives. After the Lost and Found investigation, Ms. Daniels took roll for a while tallying three items: (1) how many children came wearing gloves; (2) how many had mittens; and (3) how many were absent. For some children, it was a real discovery that the total was the same whether they counted boys-girls-absentees or mittens-gloves-absentees. When Isaiah declared that most of the glove wearers were boys, the children themselves instituted an investigation and discovered that in fact there wasn't any clear difference in the kind of hand-wear boys and girls wore.

- Do surveys that are connected to classroom investigations and that support the home–school connection, such as finding out where families go to buy groceries, or what are favorite holiday traditions.

Forms of Data Representation

As anyone who has worked in early childhood classrooms knows, young children have an endless supply of questions! However, children's questions are often hard to define, and at first they do not know how to get the data that would help them find an answer. Fortunately, these are learnable skills—but only if we adults include children in the process. If we provide children with preprinted tally sheets or charts, then we predetermine how data will be organized and children miss a vital step in learning how to manage data. In this case, graphing gets reduced to a much more limited task, such as coloring in squares on a grid.

Allowing children to sort and organize data in ways they work out for themselves engages them with the Big Ideas of data analysis. When children in Ms. Daniels's classroom complained that the winter clothes were "a big mess," she used the opportunity to help them see the need to organize the data so that they could find the answers at a glance. Experiences like this reveal the purpose of a data display and make children aware that there are important choices to be made when deciding how to represent data.

Using concrete, real objects is an essential first step in learning to represent data. Visual displays such as **object graphs** allow young children to literally see the answer when comparing sets to discover "Which has more?" as well as the more specific issue of "How many more?" without necessarily having to count. Object graphs are actually direct extensions of sorting and classifying. But, because objects can be of different sizes, it is important to help children place items in rows or in compartments on a grid for easy comparison. Teachers have found it is easy to mark off a plastic shower curtain or to use masking tape on the rug or floor to create a good framework for an object graph.

TEACHER TALK
Karina, Head Start Teacher

There are so many different cultural groups in my classroom; I'm always looking for ways to bring everyone in. We were doing an investigation of different kinds of bread as an extension of our study of *The Little Red Hen*. I asked each family to report on what kind of bread they eat most often at home. I found pictures from the food pages and magazines that the children used to create a chart showing how many families ate tortillas, pita bread, rice cakes, and sliced bread. As a result of the survey, several mothers volunteered to come in and make tortillas with the class.

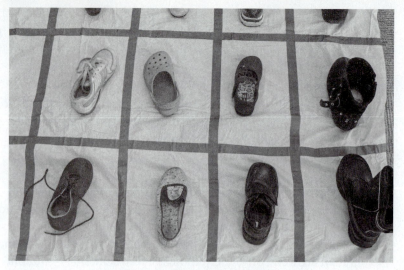

Example of an Object Graph

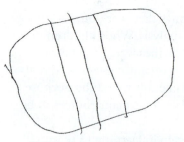

Child's Drawing of Shoe

A **pictograph** functions much the same way, but instead of using the objects themselves, each object is represented by a picture. For example, a real object shoe graph can be replaced with a pictograph by having each child draw a picture of his or her own shoe. If pictures are drawn on sticky notes, it is easy to affix them to a chart paper grid and place them in the column that reflects their "type." The sticky notes function like compartments on a grid, since they hold the vertical space between items constant. Moving from an object graph to a pictograph not only makes it possible for everyone to put their shoes back on while the data are discussed at length, but it also provides a meaningful transition between the objects themselves and a more abstract representation.

Both object graphs and pictographs display data by categories in a way that easily translates into a basic version of a **bar graph**. Data can be represented by Xs or connecting cubes or dot stickers in columns or rows labeled to show the frequency of each value. This results in a rough sketch of a bar graph. Using symbols of uniform size to "stand in" for the data, allows children to compile data on the graph in a way that creates a single set of data in each category out of many individual pieces. For example, polling students to see who prefers apples, who prefers bananas, and who prefers oranges becomes a simple matter of having each child place his connecting cube in the appropriate column; as long as the stacks of cubes are lined up fairly, a basic version of a bar graph simply emerges! Bar graphs work in a similar way as object graphs and pictographs in that the length of the different "bars" or categories can be directly compared to discover which has more.

Which Fruit Do We Prefer?

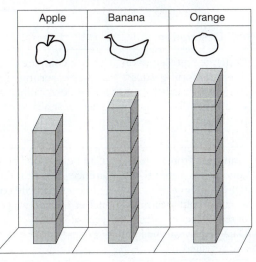

Apple	Banana	Orange

Table 7.1 lists different ways to display data that are appropriate for use in early childhood classrooms. The order in which they are given moves from more concrete to more abstract displays and describes ways to scaffold children's involvement to build understanding.

Support the Language of Data Analysis

As they create representations using objects, pictures, or graphs, children need to learn how to label and describe parts of their data displays. When children help create the labels for their own graphs, the graph and the graphing process become more meaningful. They understand that their data displays need labels and titles so that others can understand the meaning of the representation. Questions such as *How can we remember what these Xs mean?* and *What should we call this graph?* emphasize the importance of communicating to others about their graph.

Doing inventories and fact-finding surveys is a great way to support language development because children actively build meaning for key vocabulary. Collecting the data is often a hands-on activity, or picture cues can be used. For example, children can easily see where to put up their sticky note for the "How do we get to school?" survey when icons of a car, bus, bike, and walking feet label the rows. And, having children go around with a clipboard can become purposeful language practice if the survey taker is told to ask

TABLE 7.1 Ways to Display Data in Early Childhood Classrooms

Type of Graph	Description	Example	How to Involve Children in the Process
Object graph Actual objects organized into categories	• Concrete representation • Supports sorting skills • Results are easily visible, but display is not permanent	Use to compare categories after sorting of a collection of objects such as shoes or books	• Allow children to decide on the categories. • Offer a grid when children want to "get organized." • Involve children in making labels for their categories.
Pictograph Icons, drawings, or photos of objects or events organized into categories	• Transition from concrete to pictorial representation • Pictures hold meaning of real object or event • Data display can be kept and revisited	Can be used for preference or fact finding surveys—favorite color/pet or how do we get to school?	• Ask children to make their own drawings. • Children can move and reorganize drawings on sticky notes. • Label and title the graph together.
Bar graph Symbols of uniform size, such as Xs or cubes, organized into "bars" by categories	• Transition from pictorial to symbolic representation • Allows for direct visual comparison of number of items in a set without counting • Can add numbers to quantify the length of the "bars"	Good for comparing number of items in multiple sets, such as the number of birthdays each month, or for comparing data over time, such as weather	• Children compile symbols that "stand in" for the real thing to make a bar-like representation. • Emphasize the need for labels and a title to communicate meaning of graph to others. • Ask children to compare the lengths of the "bars," at first visually, then with numbers.
Tally chart Marks, or tallies, recorded by categories	• Transition from pictorial to symbolic representation • Good for keeping a running total for larger numbers • Supports grouping and idea of 5 as a "friendly" number	Use for inventories, such as contents of the Lost and Found box, or for a child-directed survey routine	• Younger children can use simple marks or checks to record data. • Support children to group tallies by 5s for easy counting. • After modeling and practice, many 4- to 6-year-olds can conduct surveys of classmates.

the same question: "How did you come to school today?" and respondents are expected to complete a sentence stem such as "I came to school today by . . . ."

The graphs and charts that represent the collected data results are also highly visual; as children join in analyzing the data, both they and the teacher can point and use other gestures while they talk about why one category might be larger or which category has the same number. And, when a data activity addresses a question or a problem that the children see as genuine and interesting, they are highly motivated to join in the discussion—another advantage for getting children talking.

Finding Great Math in Great Books

Books that inspire children to think about data are often nonfiction books. Picture books that provide lots of examples of different kinds of things can be a great way to get children thinking about a particular category of items. Any text that helps bring the complexity of the real world into the classroom can be a rich springboard for data collection and analysis. Below are some examples we have enjoyed.

- In the chapter on Sets we mentioned *Shoes, Shoes, Shoes* by Ann Morris as a great way to start a Shoe Sort activity that naturally extends into data analysis. Other wonderful picture books about shoes include *Whose Shoes? A Shoe for Every Job* by Stephen Swinburne, and *Whose Shoes Are These? A Look at Workers' Footwear—Slippers, Sneakers, and Boots* by Laura Salas. The wonderful *Pete the Cat* books by Eric Litwin could inspire another survey as to what color of shoe children likes best—especially since the underlying message is that even if we love our white shoes, we can love red, blue, or brown shoes just as well.

- William Steig's *Which Would You Rather Be?* offers a wonderfully creative set of choices. Clearly there is no right answer to "Which would you rather be, an elbow or a knee?"—but we are all interested in the unique reason people have for thinking as they do. *The Best Part of Me: Children Talk about Their Bodies in Pictures and Words* by Wendy Ewald features photos and comments by middle school children, but the idea behind this picture book works well for younger children.

- All those classrooms that schedule a fall field trip to pick apples or pumpkins are ripe for data activity. One set of questions could look at who picked how many and of what variety. The book *Apples* by Gail Gibbons talks about different varieties of apples and could be used as part of a taste testing/preference survey to extend children's thinking.

▶ Video Link

As you watch the video clip *Shoe Graph*, here are some points to reflect on.

1. In what ways does this graphing activity focus on understanding the purpose of collecting data?

2. What are ways that you see these teachers giving ownership of the lesson to the children?

3. How do the teachers help children make connections between more and less concrete data displays?

4. What evidence do you see that children are engaged and are actively constructing their own understanding of the data?

5. How does your classroom compare to that shown in the video? In what ways will you tailor or adjust your graphing activities to emphasis the Big Ideas in data analysis?

Chapter 8

SPATIAL RELATIONSHIPS
Mapping the World Around Us

Big Ideas about Spatial Relationships

- Relationships between objects and places can be described with mathematical precision.
- Our own experiences of space and two-dimensional representations of space reflect a specific point of view.
- Spatial relationships can be visualized and manipulated mentally.

Math Snapshot

It is center time in Mrs. Turner's junior kindergarten room. Jolynne, Sasha, Anthony, and Henry have gathered unit blocks, wooden railroad track pieces, and a host of zoo animals in the block corner. They announce they are going to build the train ride they took around the zoo during a class field trip last week. Jolynne and Sasha are working on enclosures for the zoo animals. "Sasha, you do the wild cats up in the corner near the shelf and I'll put the monkey house over here on this side of the tracks," Jolynne suggests.

In the meantime, Anthony and Henry are discussing the railroad track. "Remember, the track has to go straight and then curve four times to get all the way around," Anthony points out. Henry says, "I'm going to do the bridge part when the train goes over the road. That comes just past one of the curves."

Understanding spatial relationships begins at birth. Infants are learning to reach for and then grasp objects that are dangled in front of them, tossed to the side, or that have fallen down from a chair. Toddlers are crawling, cruising, or walking to reach a toy, to negotiate a path through the daycare room to rush over to Daddy at pick-up time, or to retrieve a stuffed animal from under the table. By the time they are preschoolers, not only can children easily locate items or decide how best to get from here to there; they also have begun to *represent* space:

- By describing relationships between objects and locations with words and gestures; and
- By drawing maps and constructing models, as with blocks.

While the scene from Mrs. Turner's classroom seems very familiar to anyone who lives or works with young children, many of us may not have thought of this kind of activity as being mathematical. We tend to associate mathematics primarily with numbers and operations—so that it may seem surprising to realize that things like moving through space, setting up a "tea party," telling someone where you left your towel, and building a house out of blocks are foundational experiences of geometry.

The key concepts embedded in these activities that make them mathematical are their **relational** nature. In order to work in, describe, or model space, we must manage *relationships between objects and places*, controlling positions to account for angles and lengths. Later on in mathematics, children will learn to apply numbers to such activities, measuring distances and angles, and learning the meaning of "parallel" and "equilateral," but for now, their efforts will be focused on more general ways to represent relationships between objects and places.

Children between the ages of 3 and 6 are more than ready to develop their skills at expressing directions from different locations and understanding relative positions. They are fundamentally interested in modeling their world, whether in the block corner or the housekeeping area, and spatial relationships are a large part of what they grapple with there. The more such experiences they have, particularly in the company of adults who help to *mathematize* them, the easier it will be to make their own representations of space mathematically precise when they get to geometry class. These early experiences talking about, organizing, moving through, drawing, and modeling space provide a critical conceptual base for the mathematical study that will turn them into engineers, architects, scientists, taxi cab drivers, and other adults who competently make their way from here to there.

We have identified three Big Ideas in the topic of spatial relationships that you can use to inform the foundational experiences in mathematics you provide for children.

- Young children who understand the first Big Idea—that *relationships between objects and places can be represented with mathematical precision*—know that "where" something is can be conveyed by talking, drawing, writing, and creating models to **represent** movement and direction.

- When young children are exposed to the second Big Idea—that *our own experiences of space and two-dimensional representations of space reflect a specific point of view*—they begin to develop an awareness of **perspective**, that is, the understanding that spatial relationships look different when viewed from different positions. It will take time before they understand that when they are face to face with their friend, something on *their left* appears to their friend on *her right*, but early experiences can prepare them for this type of sophisticated thinking.

- Children who are aware of the third Big Idea—that *spatial relationships can be visualized and manipulated mentally*—are learning how to hold a spatial representation in their "mind's eye." This important and useful skill can be challenging for young learners, but they build proficiency when we provide many concrete and pictorial experiences with spatial **transformations**, such as cutting an item in half, flipping it upside down, or rotating it to make it "fit."

Early childhood classrooms, then, need to provide many types of opportunities to talk about, draw, and model spatial relationships, allowing children to notice different perspectives and imagine the results of spatial transformations. In this chapter, we will try to help you see what is important about each of these kinds of experiences, and how you can enrich them and help connect them to the mathematical thinking of your young students. We hope you will become convinced that geometric thinking is one of the most natural—and most exciting—ways for young children to explore the mathematics that is all around us.

 ## Big Idea: Relationships between Objects and Places Can Be Represented with Mathematical Precision

Math Snapshot

When Mrs. Turner sees how deeply engaged Henry, Sasha, Jolynne, and Anthony are by their construction, she unobtrusively takes several photos. She also notes some of the language they use to coordinate—or negotiate—how the construction will go. Anthony and Henry have agreed on the area that their track will enclose; now they are trying to decide which pieces of track to use. "Don't use that piece," Henry says. "It has to curve this way here, so it can go around the loop and come back to the station."

In the meantime, Jolynne and Sasha are discussing their enclosures. Jolynne wants to know why Sasha has placed the monkey house so close to the penguins. "The penguins are supposed to be next to the lions!"

"The penguins are scared of the lions, so I put the monkeys in between them. The monkeys aren't scared."

Block play is not always this sophisticated. First, as all early childhood professionals know, children move through many kinds of social play before they engage with each other in a truly cooperative style. Moreover, 3-year-olds and young 4-year-olds need time to experiment with blocks, laying out roads, seeing how blocks can make enclosures, and eventually building bridges. Once these basic structural ideas are in place, children can begin to use these tools to create a model of the world they are learning so much about every day. Having a mixed-age group can help this occur, since older children with more block experience and verbal skills are more likely to use blocks to create specific worlds. But there are also things teachers can do to encourage the representational use of blocks, such as including small play figures and cars in the block area, or putting up posters of buildings to give children ideas. All block play that involves combining blocks is useful, but representational block play has a special advantage in promoting analytical thought about spatial relationships.

Mrs. Turner knows that a digital camera is a valuable tool for documenting children's work, and often uses photos on bulletin boards and as part of ongoing assessments of children's learning. Today, however, she plans to use her photos to make a more direct contribution to the children's learning, helping them revisit what they did and reflect on it.

Photos are particularly useful when the subject is spatial relationships. Photos can capture an image of the space between objects and places, allowing children to contemplate it in isolation, remember it clearly, and compare it to other images of space in a way that other media can't quite match. In real life, spatial relationships often change, as when a chair is moved to a different table, or the blocks are put away for use again tomorrow. A photo is a simple way to create a shared visual representation of a space that can be thoughtfully discussed again and again.

For young children, the key to getting the math out of looking at representations of places and objects—such as photographs—is discussion. Teachers of young children need to help them develop vocabulary for describing spatial relationships. There are endless "math all around us" opportunities to support this critical aspect of language development for all children.

A simple reminding remark such as "Where do we keep the paintbrushes?" is an opportunity for children to describe their understanding of space. If the response is a gesture or a phrase such as "over here," you can take advantage by saying, "that's right, we keep them *in* the coffee can *on* the shelf *by* the window," modeling a much more precise response. If your spatial language is rich and precise, over time, children's language will become more specific, as will their understanding.

Mrs. Turner openly admits that it took her a while to realize that these directional and positional words are actually mathematical. She remembers realizing that we often use a string of descriptors and how each term describes a specific spatial relationship. For example, the relationship between the paintbrushes and the coffee can is that the paintbrushes are *in* the coffee can. The relationship between the coffee can and the shelf is that the coffee can is *on* the shelf. By stringing all these relationships together, we use language to give a very specific set of spatial directions.

Young children usually are not capable of constructing long strings of spatial descriptors, but by preschool, they find effective ways to communicate what is needed, and block play is likely to encourage them to do so. So while Henry's "that piece" and "curve this way" are rather imprecise when you are not in the room to see his gestures, his "go around the loop and come back to the station" gives a very clear picture of where the track must go. Jolynne's "next to the lions" and Sasha's "in between them" are both very effective descriptions of spatial relationships, making their ideas crystal clear. While individual block play has a strong spatial component all on its own, when children are required to negotiate and discuss their creations, the need to represent their spatial thinking in words drives the mathematical content to new levels of complexity.

Math Snapshot

Mrs. Turner created a small display of the artifacts the children collected from the zoo trip in an area of the classroom she titled "Adventures." The four children bring Mrs. Turner the map the zoo had provided of its train circuit. They want to create a map of their zoo, complete with all its improvements. Mrs. Turner lets them know that the map is a great idea; she works to get them started but does so as a shared experience, with her holding the pencil but leaving decisions to the children. She also gathers the photos of the zoo structure she had snapped earlier. She explains that first she will create a larger outline of the whole zoo's outer walls, then comments, "Now that we know how much space the whole zoo includes, should I draw the train track next? How far into the middle should I put it?"

The children crowd around Mrs. Turner making suggestions. They look back at the photos to help them. At times she hands the pencil over to them so that they can show her what they think should go where.

Mrs. Turner is very aware that being able to *name* and verbally describe locations and spatial relationships is not the only way to show and develop understanding. Drawing pictures and maps and moving through space are equally legitimate and important ways to *represent* movement and direction. In fact, for many children whose language is not fully developed, these other representations are the best place to begin. Mrs. Turner knows she can use these alternative modes to reinforce the language children need. This mapping exercise is especially rich, because the children first modeled the zoo with blocks, using spatial language to coordinate their efforts, and now will use a map to redescribe the same set of spatial relationships in another way.

So as children point and talk about *over here, on this side, on that side*, Mrs. Turner echoes and clarifies by talking about *on the right, on the left, next to*, and *across from* while mimicking their gestures to be sure she understands. She also pushes the children to be as specific as possible about relationships between locations as they puzzle out how to accurately draw things that are *really close* as opposed to those that are *pretty far from each other*.

She knows that they are not developmentally able to get as specific as adults are and to establish a *scale* so that one inch on the map equals one block, one mile, 10 miles, or 100 miles. But the more experience they have with mapping their environments—such as their bedrooms, their classroom, or the path they take to school—the more they are honing their sense of how to represent spatial relationships and preparing to understand geometry.

TEACHER TALK
Sara, Kindergarten Bilingual Classroom Teacher

My husband is from Mexico; I feel quite fluent in Spanish, but I can still get tripped up by words like *in front of—de frente; behind—detrás; the side of—al lado de; over—encima;* and *under—y bajo.* I've learned that prepositions—words that describe spatial relationships between objects—are particularly difficult to master, for me, as well as for the kids. I try to be really clear about how I use them in English.

Movement games are another important way to help children think about and understand space. Song games and dances, in which children move in specific ways in response to directions, such as "put your right hand *in*" in the Hokey Pokey, or "we all fall *down*" in Ring Around the Rosy, provide a fun way to help children develop their listening skills while they get movement and direction literally into their bodies. *Simon Says* and *Captain May I?* are other examples of games that require children to concentrate on listening, and the group aspect of these activities supports those who are uncertain about what different words mean in a fun and exciting way. Older children will enjoy being the leader of such activities, and coming up with new ideas for *where* children should put their bodies.

There are also many books that lend themselves well to being re-created as obstacle courses in the classroom. *Rosie's Walk* by Pat Hutchins and *We are Going on a Bear Hunt* by Michael Rosen, for example, are stories about journeys that take their participants past, through, over, and across many different objects and places. Acting such stories out can be a springboard to creating your own "bear hunt," that goes "*past* the art center, *through* the block area, *over* the reading rug, and *across* the hall."

Big Idea: Our Own Experiences of Space and Two-Dimensional Representations of Space Reflect a Specific Point of View

Math Snapshot

Mrs. Turner allows the children to study the pictures of the zoo and comment for a bit; then she says, "What can you tell me about how you decided where different things would go?"

Henry is quick to respond, making a sweeping motion over the photo with his hand. "We knew we wanted to fill the whole block area because the zoo is big. And we wanted the train to go all around the middle so there could be animals inside and outside."

"Animals inside and outside?" Mrs. Turner repeats and looks thoughtful. Jolynne jumps in, "See, if the train went around all the way next to the walls, it wouldn't be fair. If you had to sit on the outside part of the train, you wouldn't be able to see anything but the wall. But if the track is more in the middle, both sides get to see the animals." As she is talking, she is pointing to the left and then the right side of the one train car visible in the picture. Anthony nods vigorously and adds, "That's why Daddy never puts the car seats in the middle. Both me and my sister want to see!"

"So you all agreed that the train track should go all the way around but there should be animals both on the right and on the left of the track," says Mrs. Turner, taking the opportunity to model more specific directional language. "At first I was wondering if you meant that some animals would be inside their areas and other animals would be outside." After a pause, Henry says, "At the petting zoo, we were all 'inside' with the animals!"

In this situation, because the children are discussing their own experience of the zoo spaces, their language reflects an added level of complexity, involving point of view, or **perspective**. When we are in the scenario ourselves, we become part of the spatial relationships, and then position and location are always described relative to ourselves. Young children do not need to be able to explain this, but they need lots of experience talking about how things appear from their own point of view, and hearing how they appear from someone else's.

The ability to truly **de-center** and think about how something looks from someone else's point of view takes time to come into place—it cannot be taught, or forced. But rich experiences and language that makes this fact of our spatial experiences clear helps children solidify their thinking. Similarly, children need extensive practice with slippery concepts such as *right* and *left*, though these ideas, too, will mature on their own schedule.

There are many situations in life that involve two-dimensional representations of space. Children's drawings always reflect a particular perspective on a spatial situation, but this is not usually obvious to them. When children draw an object, there is an implicit choice, usually determined by convention, about the perspective from which it will be drawn.

Drawing a house as seen from the street, or a person as though he is standing and facing you, are almost universal assumptions based on our experiences of the world. Most children learn how to draw these types of images by imitating the work of older or more practiced peers. When children know how to visually represent these objects, they gain a sense of how powerfully two-dimensional drawings can convey ideas, spatial and otherwise. A map, however, while still two-dimensional, is most usefully drawn from above, a "bird's-eye" perspective that is not a regular part of our real-world experience—unless we are looking down at a creation in the block corner like the children's zoo. This makes maps much more difficult for young children to understand.

Maps do have the special advantage, however, of being explicitly tied to real-world experiences. The children in Mrs. Turner's class were very interested in the zoo map in part because they had actually been to the zoo. It was natural to them to try to compare and connect their lived, three-dimensional experience to this two-dimensional representation, an exercise that can support their developing understanding of perspective.

To help young children accomplish this difficult task, it can be effective to have them draw their own "map" based on a sequence of direct experiences, such as a walk. By recalling with children what they saw on their walk through the school's neighborhood, and then asking, "Which thing did we come to first? The playground, or the store?" teachers can help children represent "next to," in two dimensions. Classroom obstacle courses, too, are ideal for mapping—especially when they have been created by children in the first place. While maps produced through this process don't always accurately depict spatial relationships, they are an important step toward later, more complex representations.

Math Snapshot

Mrs. Turner decides that she will focus the mid-year family math night on geometry. Building off of the zoo map activity, she will have children and their parents work together to create a map of the classroom, using an 11" × 17" piece of paper with the classroom walls, windows, and door sketched in. Each family group will be given a few easily recognizable items cut out of construction paper to place in the room, such as Mrs. Turner's rocking chair, the rug, the classroom sink, the easels, and the playhouse. Realizing that map-making is a very complex process, and she wants the children to take a leading role, she models it first for the whole group.

"Now where does the rocking chair go? By the rug is right . . . is this the right place?" she asks. "No, no!" shouts Peri, "it's not on the sink side of the rug, it's on the door side of the rug!" "Oh," says Mrs. Turner, "so it goes by the rug, across from the sink, and next to the door. Does that look right?"

Map of the Classroom

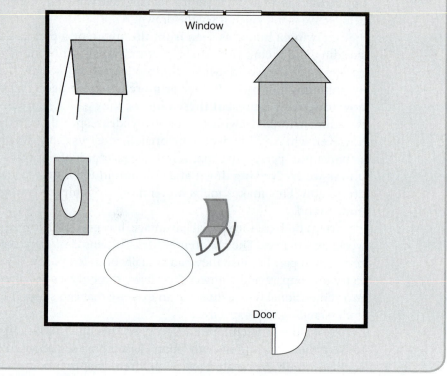

Big Idea: Spatial Relationships Can Be Visualized and Manipulated Mentally

Math Snapshot

In addition to posters that show the children's block constructions and drawings, on family math night Mrs. Turner puts out a variety of puzzles for children to demonstrate and parents to try. She smiles to see Jan pulling his mother over to the pattern block templates. Though Jan's English is very much at the early emergent stage, he is the class whiz when it comes to these puzzles. Jan is chattering in Polish as he chooses a template that gives only an outline of the shape, then quickly fills in the design using two small triangles, three trapezoids, and one hexagon; then he grins up at his mother, sweeps away the pieces and rapidly does the shape again, using eight diamonds and one small triangle. Mrs. Turner loves watching how he will hold a piece up and look at it and back at the space in the puzzle and then flip or change the orientation.

Nearby, Ida is coaching her 2-year-old brother as he tries to put the three pigs' houses into a wooden peg puzzle. He has one of the shapes by the knob and is randomly banging it on the puzzle. "Turn it around, Andy," she urges and when he continues smashing, she takes the piece, turns it and slips it in, saying, "See, turn it around just like I did." But Andreas has lost interest and heads for his mother. Ida sighs, "He's just a little kid. I guess he'll get it when he's older."

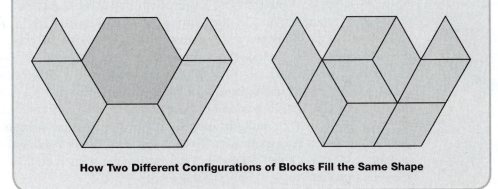

How Two Different Configurations of Blocks Fill the Same Shape

Both Jan and Ida are demonstrating that they have taken yet another step in their understanding of spatial relationships. Not only can they express and represent spatial relationships by constructing them, they also clearly have developed *mental images* that allow them to see how flipping or turning a shape can lead to a solution. Jan's confidence that he can complete the pattern block template in more than one way leads him to persevere, turning blocks one way and another until every space is perfectly filled. Ida can look at the space on the puzzle board and find a contour that is repeated on the puzzle piece—you just have to turn it a bit first!

In each case, the children are imagining what these shapes will look like when they are spatially manipulated.

Mrs. Turner knows that Ida is quite right: Andreas is much too young for this kind of mental representation. "And let's face it," she thinks ruefully to herself, "I still have trouble figuring out how to pack the car trunk." Mental transformation of objects and spaces is difficult for many of us, but we all use at least some of this skill set all the time, as we shift our wrist to set the portable phone down properly in its charger, or even figure out the most efficient way to load the dishwasher.

There is evidence that practice can make a difference; in fact, athletes and musicians have each been shown to have enhanced mental rotation skills. It is theorized this is because athletes spend so much time moving their bodies thoughtfully and effectively through space, and because music is written using spatial notation. Regardless, mental transformational skills are used by mechanics, brain surgeons, engineers, chefs, welders, and sculptors every day. Providing young children with many opportunities to complete puzzles, draw pictures, solve mazes, build with unit blocks, tinker toys, and hollow blocks, dance, make things out of clay, and navigate outdoor climbing structures gives children practice imagining and mentally manipulating spaces.

 ## Implications for Teaching

The early childhood classroom is bursting with opportunities for children to explore spatial relationships. Whether through their bodies, through language, with blocks, with paint and paper, with puzzles, or in the housekeeping area, space is the medium in which children (and all of us!) operate, so it is not difficult to find it as part of a young child's day. What is difficult, however, is the teacher's job: knowing how and when to scaffold and push children's understanding, having ideas for how to focus children's attention on those parts of spatial concepts that are tricky for them, and providing multiple opportunities to explore and manipulate space through many different modalities. To help you think about making these choices in your classroom, Table 8.1 describes how to begin and then build on understanding in several key types of spatial activities.

Support the Language of Spatial Relationships

The development of children's informal sense of space into the kind of mathematical understanding involved in geometry is inseparable from language development. When we apply language to spatial relationships, we force greater precision, making clear distinctions between *over* and *next to*, and between *curved* and *straight*. It is also true, however, that in assessing children's knowledge of spatial relationships, just as in all areas of mathematics, we need to recognize receptive understanding; that is, children who cannot describe a space verbally nonetheless perceive it and can move through or manipulate it. Encourage

TABLE 8.1   Activities That Build Understanding of Spatial Relationships

Activity/Task	At First	As Understanding and Skill Develop
Blocks and Other Construction Materials *Examples* Unit blocks Plastic bricks Magnetic tiles	Children always need plenty of time for free exploration with materials. When introducing different kinds of building materials such as magnetic tiles, take time to discuss how each material has special qualities but also may have some limitations.	Periodically introduce challenges such as, *How many different ways can you use these 10 blocks to build something?* *How high a tower can you build? Can you use a different material to build a higher one?* Encourage children to sketch plans and make drawings of constructions they have completed. Use photos to document work and invite the children to write or dictate descriptions.
Movement Songs and Games *Examples* Hokey Pokey Captain May I? Simon Says	Do not force children to sing along or chant words until they are comfortable doing so. Keep the pace slow at first and look for indications that the children understand what movement is expected. Just before or after a round, use gesture to remind children about *left* and *right* and other tricky terms.	As children become increasingly familiar with the games and songs, have them take turns being the leader or calling out the directions.
Informal Games and Activities *Examples* Where Is It? Doggie, Doggie, Where's My Bone? Hide and Seek	A child hides a treasured classroom object, such as a stuffed bear; she then uses words to tell others where to look, saying "It's *near* the doorway," and "It's on the side *opposite of* the clock." When the "hider" needs help describing the location, the teacher can ask questions, such as "Is it *closer* to the block corner, or the rug?"	As the children become more fluent with positional language, prompt them to use increasingly precise language: "Is it *behind* the chair or is it *beneath* it?" Challenge children to describe an object's location with two or more position words: "It's *on* the floor and *next to* the table."
Obstacle Courses and Mapping Activities	Model the route through an obstacle course, pairing movements with words, such as "Go *past* the bookshelf; jump *over* the block," and so on. Have all the children join in chanting the directions as each child goes through the course.	In time, children will enjoy setting up their own obstacle courses. Have children create a path through the classroom that represents the movement in a story such as *Rosie's Walk* by Pat Hutchins or Little Red Riding Hood's route from her house to her grandmother's. Go on to get them to draw these paths as maps.
Puzzles *Examples* Jigsaw puzzles Pattern blocks Tangrams	Doing puzzles involves dexterity as well as spatial sense. Children who come to school with experience doing puzzles will be ready to do puzzles with more pieces earlier than those who are just beginning. Introduce special forms such as pattern blocks and tangrams by modeling while you "think aloud" to explain your strategies.	Multi-piece puzzles, pattern blocks, and tangrams should be available with different levels of support. Begin tangrams and pattern-block puzzles with those that have a few simple shapes and a clear outline of each shape. Gradually move on to those that only provide an outline and have multiple solutions.

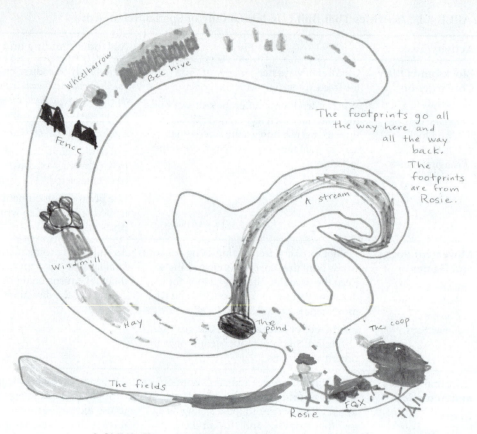

The footprints go all the way here and all the way back.

The footprints are from Rosie.

Wheelbarrow

Bee hive

Fence

A stream

Windmill

Hay

The pond

The coop

The fields

Rosie

Fox

A Child's Map with Dictation Based on *Rosie's Walk* by Pat Hutchins

young children to use gestures, movements, and other forms of representation to describe spatial relationships. Observe and support these indications of understanding, seizing opportunities to model the use of rich and specific language. Having children talk with a partner and then share with the group can also be a good way to provide safe opportunities to try out the language of spatial relationships.

Position words tend to be heavily influenced by context—their exact meanings sometimes don't translate directly from one language to another. Because of this, the words we use in English to describe spatial relationships can seem arbitrary and be especially difficult for English Language Learners to master. For example, while in English a child may be "next" in line, in Spanish, he is "el siguiente." On the other hand, if the plant is "next to" the fish tank, it is "al lado de" in Spanish. If you have many children who are learning English in your class, it will be especially important to present position words with lots of visual and kinesthetic support, and to explicitly connect real-world spaces and locations with the words that describe them.

Harness the Power of Block Building

As Mrs. Turner's classroom shows us, building with blocks provides a powerful, playful way for children to explore spatial relationships. We believe every early childhood classroom should be well-stocked with blocks and plentiful space and time for building.

TEACHER TALK

Addy, Pre-K Inclusion Classroom Teacher

I think it's important to make the point to parents and administrators that the block corner and all the music and movement games we do are how I teach, and the children learn, mathematics. I keep telling them, if the kids don't have the math in their hands and bodies, it will never get into their heads!

Table 8.2 describes the types of structures that children are likely to build, from the most basic to the more advanced. Of course, experience makes a big difference, and children who come to school with prior blocks experience, or who are older, move quickly through the early stages. Do not consider these stages as a checklist of skills, but rather as a guide to help you recognize the types of

TABLE 8.2   Stages of Block Building*

Stage	What Children Can Do
Discovery	Children carry, move, touch, hold, pile, knock down, and drop the blocks. Children do little or no building.
Towers and Roads	Children stack blocks vertically or line them up in rows horizontally. Children will often repeat a pattern over and over.
Bridges	Children form a space between two blocks and place a third block on top to make a bridge or doorway. Children begin to explore balance and rotate blocks to use their widths and ends of the blocks.
Enclosures	Children can close up a space between blocks with another block(s) to make walls, fences, rooms, cages, and so on. Children often like to add figures, such as animals or cars.
Patterns and Symmetry	Children make more elaborate, decorative structures, using pattern and symmetry. Children often sort and match blocks' shapes and sizes.
Representational Building	Structures often reproduce or symbolize actual buildings or places the children know. Children begin to plan ahead and often want to build and play with a structure over a period of several days.

*Based on *The Block Book*, edited by Elisabeth S. Hirsch (NAEYC, 1996, rev. ed.).

buildings children make and to know what kinds of structures to encourage them to try building next.

Ensure Equal Access for Girls and Boys

Gender differences in spatial ability, which emerge before the time children enter kindergarten, are largely due to differences in experience and expectations. For all young children, opportunities to move their bodies through space are foundational for later success in spatial thinking tasks. Thus, we must give girls as well as boys many opportunities to climb monkey bars, play hide and seek, go on treasure hunts, and run around the bases at recess. Some girls may need encouragement to play with blocks or other construction materials; including dramatic play props such as toy animals and people in the block corner can make it more inviting to girls. Because girls might not gravitate themselves to the kinds of play that develop visual–spatial skills, we need to be mindful that both girls and boys have the opportunity to participate.

As we know from previous chapters, spatial relationships are central to visual patterns, measurement, data displays, and the knowledge of shapes discussed in the next chapter. We've also seen that spatial thinking is critical for building subitizing skills and more advanced counting strategies. Thus, attention to spatial relationships should be woven throughout the mathematics curriculum and throughout the children's day.

Finding Great Math in Great Books

- The spare text of *Rosie's Walk* by Pat Hutchins focuses on position words and invites dramatizing the tale as an obstacle course. The same author's *Changes, Changes* is wordless but the pictures show how a single set of building blocks can be transformed to tell an exciting adventure story.
- Most early childhood teachers have a great repertoire of action songs and games, but for a multicultural touch you might want to consult collections such as *Skip Across the Ocean*, collected by Floella Benjamin or *Acka Backa Boo*, collected by Opal Dunn. Also, there are traditional stories or activities such as *Going on a Bear Hunt*.
- *Block City*, Daniel Kirk's illustrated version of the Robert Louis Stevenson poem, offers rich opportunities for children to discuss and express spatial relationships. *Building a House* by Byron Barton and Ann Morris's *Houses and Homes*, as well Anna Grifalcone's *The Village of Round Houses and Square Houses*, are other picture books that can stimulate conversation and building projects.
- *Me on a Map* by Joan Sweeney is a great informational picture book that introduces mapping to young children. *From Here to There* by Maria Cuyler and *Where Do I Live?* by Neil Chesnow are easily understandable picture books that gradually expand from the child's place in her own bedroom to the universe.

 # Video Link

As you watch the video clip *Walk with Rosie*, here are some points to reflect on:

1. How does the sequence of activities support children to represent their understanding of spatial relationships in more than one way?

2. How does this teacher give ownership of the lesson to the children?

3. List the ways this teacher supports children's language development?

4. What evidence do you see that children are engaged and are actively constructing their own understanding?

5. How does your classroom compare to that shown in the video? In what ways will you tailor or adjust the activity to meet your children's needs and interests?

Chapter 9

SHAPE
Developing Definitions

Math Snapshot

Mr. Barry is beginning an exploration of geometry in his kindergarten classroom. At the end of morning group time, he brings out a large basket of wooden shapes collected from the assortment of unit blocks and geometric solids (cones, spheres, and hemispheres) that are available in the block area. He holds up a few of the shapes as he announces, "I have been noticing how many of you are experts at building complicated structures with different kinds of blocks. I think you are ready to really think about what makes one shape good for a certain kind of structure and not so good another time."

"We will start our investigation on shapes as soon as you get back to your tables. I am going to come around and give each of you one wooden shape. Look at it carefully and then compare it with the others at your table. Work together to make a poster about your set of shapes."

Everything in the material world has shape. However, in mathematics, the focus is very much on regular shapes, such as the two-dimensional circle, triangle, and rectangle (including everyone's favorite rectangle, the square) and the three-dimensional solids known as spheres and **polyhedrons** (that is, geometric solids with flat faces and straight edges). In our everyday world, these solids commonly appear in objects we describe as boxes, pyramids, blocks, cylinders, and balls.

Many adults have only a very basic knowledge of shape. For example, not everyone knows how to recognize a right triangle, an equilateral triangle, or an isosceles triangle—let alone how you decide whether a trapezoid is also a quadrilateral! Three-dimensional shapes are even more of a mystery, since many of us do not know how to distinguish a triangular prism from a triangular pyramid.

As a teacher of young children, you don't need an extremely technical understanding of these things, but you do need to know more than most. A deeper knowledge about how two- and three-dimensional shapes are defined and relate to one another will help you be aware of subtle distinctions and rules. Such an understanding will allow you to notice and highlight children's key discoveries, and to guide their experiences to make this knowledge explicit for them. To help you develop your own knowledge about shapes—and to provide a reference for you as you read through this chapter—we have provided a "primer" on shapes in the Implications for Teaching section in Table 9.2. Feel free to skip ahead and refer to it if you have questions about a shape as you read through, to help clarify your thinking.

The block corner is particularly rich in the mathematics of shape—both two- and three-dimensional! Time children spend playing with blocks and other materials familiarizes them with important geometric ideas and prepares them to become analytical about and creative with shape. Blocks are a naturally engaging way to involve children's eyes, ears, hands, and whole body directly and actively with geometric thinking. The kind of thoughtful guided inquiry Mr. Barry is bringing to the children's block play will develop their understanding of shapes, and will eventually touch upon three distinct Big Ideas we believe ought to guide the teaching of young children:

- Children need to go beyond the use of superficial shape labels to recognizing and specifying the defining attributes of shapes. As children sort and classify shapes with knowledgeable others, they become aware of rules about shapes, such as that a triangle has three sides and three angles (corners), that a cylinder has a rounded form with two flat ends that are in the shape of a circle, or that a sphere has only one continuous curved side. That these sorts of precise distinctions can be made is not immediately obvious to young children; for this reason, it is important that teachers design activities that show them that *shapes can be defined and classified according to their attributes.*

- As they explore three-dimensional solids, children will discover for themselves that the faces (or sides) of these solids look like circles, rectangles, triangles, and other common two-dimensional shapes. They are now making sense of another Big Idea about shapes: *The flat faces of solid (three-dimensional) shapes are two-dimensional shapes.*

- Opportunities to combine, rotate, and compare shapes will help children develop understanding of part/whole relationships within and among shapes, as when two identical right triangles can be combined to make a rectangle. This concept—that there are shapes within shapes—is the basis of the Big Idea: *Shapes can be combined and separated (composed and decomposed) to make new shapes.*

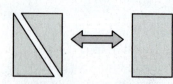

Shapes Can Be Combined

Teachers like Mr. Barry who have a strong understanding of child development realize that they are laying a foundation. Developmentally, young children
are not ready for the kind of generalizing and level of precision they will be asked
to achieve in junior high and high school geometry. However, it is essential that
they are able to see the roots of these concepts in the world all around them—and
that the habit of "mathematizing" shape is firmly in place.

Big Idea: Shapes Can Be Defined and Classified by Their Attributes

Math Snapshot

As part of the poster project, Mr. Barry gives each table drawings of the three-
dimensional shapes that they are exploring. The children are to cut and paste the
pictures from the sheet for the shapes they have and then work together to record
observations about how shapes are the same and different.

Over the course of a few days, Mr. Barry uses his guided math time to bring two
table groups at a time together to share and compare their posters as well as the
actual solids. This keeps the group to a size that will allow everyone to participate as
they describe and sort the eight shapes they are considering. Mr. Barry makes mental
notes of the language the children use. Jasmine and Zion discuss the cones they had.
"I'm pretending mine is really strawberry chocolate," Zion declares. Jasmine giggles,
"We both look like we ate all the ice cream and just have the cone left."

Cara points to a large and a small cylinder in the collection they are exploring,
"These are the same, because they are round around and have two flat sides that
look like circles. But they aren't the same because one is bigger." Mr. Barry nods in
agreement, "That's a good observation, Cara. Both of these are cylinders—that's
the name used in math talk; they are the same shape even though they are
different sizes."

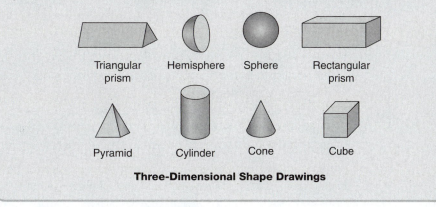

Three-Dimensional Shape Drawings

Mr. Barry is one of those wonderful early childhood teachers who truly understands constructivism. Children learn most when they make their own discoveries; they relish being "knowledge detectives" who look for clues and can explain how they use the clues to solve problems. In this introduction to geometric shapes, Mr. Barry wants the children to take the time to handle the solids and literally get a feel for their *defining attributes*. Kindergarteners should be able to sort the solids into those that are pointed, or rounded, and those that have all flat sides; he is also looking for evidence the children can match a three-dimensional shape with its representation as a drawing.

Mr. Barry has intentionally placed several different sizes of the same shapes in the collection that the children are exploring. He is particularly pleased with Cara's observation; he knows that attributes of size and color often "trump" all the others. Her remark shows that she has begun to generalize and understand that the attributes of a rounded side and two flat circular faces are what make a cylinder a cylinder, not the size, and certainly not the color.

At the early stage of exploring shapes, Mr. Barry is right to have the children focus in on the attributes rather than the technical names for the solids. English Language Learners are not the only ones who might stumble over terms like *rectangular* or *triangular prisms*. In any case, with repeated exposure and use many children will naturally shift to using terms like *cubes* or *spheres* while others continue to talk about *blocks* and *balls*.

Math Snapshot

The following Monday, Mr. Barry announces that he has a new "Math Challenge." Over the next week, up to four children at a time are to build towers, following these rules:

- The goal is to build a tower using *no more than seven* of the blocks; they have to use *at least three different shapes* and one block has to have either a pointed or rounded side.
- They can decide if they would like their tower to be "stronger" or "higher."
- Digital photos will be taken of all the completed towers and will be used to complete a tower report that is expected for each structure.

Mr. Barry knows that successfully following all these rules will be difficult for the children on their own, so he begins with a lot of guidance. He chooses four

(continued)

volunteers to model the activity; two will work on a "stronger" tower and the other two will work on one that is "higher." Once the towers are completed and photos have been taken, Mr. Barry calls on different observers to share their thoughts. He points to wide cylinders that are toward the bottom of the "stronger" tower, and asks, "Can someone tell me why they think Emerson and Avi put these shapes here in the way they did?"

Hands shoot up all over the group; others nod when Davita explains, "They might of could put it one more on top but those round towers are too big to go at the way top. And anyway, if they had turned them on the round side, everything would just roll off. They had to use the flat part down!"

One Completed Tower Report

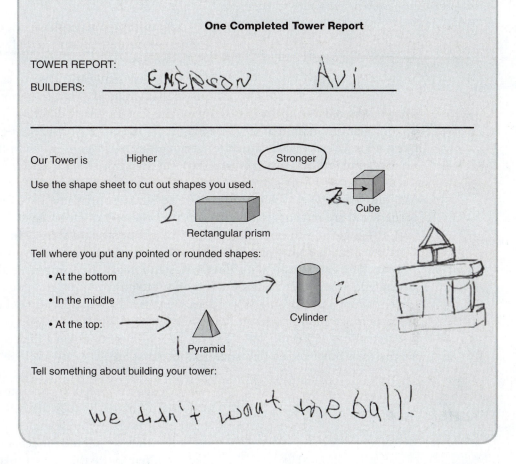

TOWER REPORT:

BUILDERS: ___ENERSON___ ___AVI___

_____

Our Tower is   Higher   (Stronger)

Use the shape sheet to cut out shapes you used.

Rectangular prism — Cube

Tell where you put any pointed or rounded shapes:

• At the bottom

• In the middle

• At the top: Pyramid   Cylinder

Tell something about building your tower:

We didn't want the ball!

It's springtime now, and the children in this classroom have learned much about being members of a learning community. They know that this is not a contest, with winners and losers. Instead, they have learned challenges are much more interesting and, in the end, more fun because everyone gets to see so many different ways to solve an interesting problem.

Mr. Barry has intentionally designed this challenge; the constraints on the number and types of solids the children can use will focus the kindergarteners on the *defining attributes of shapes*. At the same time, it draws their attention to the way that three-dimensional shapes can have a variety of differently shaped *faces;* that the solids can be rotated and oriented in different ways, and that the number and shape of these faces enter into the defining attributes of a solid.

By putting the emphasis on the defining attributes, children avoid common misconceptions about what triangles or rectangles actually are. They develop awareness that while all *rectangles* are made of *four straight sides and four square corners*, rectangles can look very different, depending on their orientation and on the lengths of the sides. Some rectangles look like a door with two sides much longer than the other two, and with the long sides oriented up and down (vertically). But the same shape is still a rectangle if the two parallel long sides are shown as the "top" and "bottom." A rhombus has four sides as well, which must all be equal, but only some have four square corners and are rectangles. Squares, on the other hand, meet the definition of both rectangle and rhombus, since they have four straight sides, which are of equal length, and four square (or 90 degree) corners. Sometimes young children will see these relationships for themselves and might, for example, call a square a rectangle. When this occurs, it's important to affirm rather than deny this understanding, perhaps by saying "yes, a square is a very special kind of rectangle, because all four sides are the same length." When we rely on a superficial understanding of "rectangle," however, based on ideas such as "like a door," we can miss other rectangles, such as those that are "like an envelope" or "like a washcloth." We also rob children of the knowledge they need to generate real working definitions of shapes that will extend usefully into later mathematics.

So while we should model and encourage children to use the correct mathematical terms for shapes, we should be equally vigilant that they understand that number of sides, lengths of sides, and size of angles are key features, and that the "rules" for how they appear are different for each type of shape.

Diverse Shape Examples

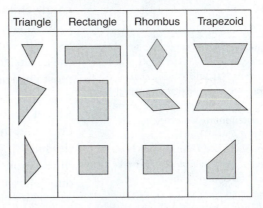

Triangle	Rectangle	Rhombus	Trapezoid

Big Idea: The Flat Faces of Solid (Three-Dimensional) Shapes Are Two-Dimensional Shapes

Math Snapshot

The Tower Math Challenge has been a great success. At Friday group time Mr. Barry asks for ideas about what he should include in the Challenge Report Newsletter he will send home.

Emerson and a few other fervent builders have begun to make a tally of which kind of shapes get used most often. He is clearly excited as he announces, "I looked and double checked and not one single tower has a ball in it! Nobody wanted it, just like me and Avi didn't the first time."

Mr. Barry rephrases using the mathematical term, "Emerson is saying that no one used a sphere to make a tower? Did anyone else notice that?" Quite a few of the children nod in agreement. Henry is among the first to comment, "Me and Ellie tried to use it but there wasn't any way to make it go onto a tower because it's round all over."

Pete says, "We put that half circle/ball on the top of our tower. It works because it does have a flat side."

Avi says, "But it has to be on the top, because the rest of it is round."

Mr. Barry follows up by asking, "Did anyone notice what shape the flat side of the hemisphere looks like?" "It's a circle! And guess what, the cone and the slinder one have flat circles, too!" Tyrone announces.

Mr. Barry smiles, "You all are making so many good observations. I'm having a hard time keeping up with you. So, Tyrone, are you saying that the hemisphere and the cylinder both have flat sides that look like circles?" When Tyrone and others nod in agreement, Mr. Barry explains, "There is a special word for the flat sides of three-dimensional shapes. They are called *faces*. As you noticed, these faces are the shapes we know, like circles and rectangles."

The other day, I was sitting with a few of the younger children as they were playing with play-dough. Nina had rolled hers flat and looked at it for a moment; then she picked up one of the small geometric solids from a basket and started pressing different faces into it. Tommy was fascinated and kept naming the shapes—"That block made a square! That one made a circle! That made a triangle!" Then he started using other blocks to make more shapes. I did take the opportunity to point out that the flat sides of the solids are the shapes we usually talk about—but it was so exciting to see how the children had made the discovery for themselves.

All too often, teachers and parents of young children focus on getting children to learn labels for shapes by rote through use of flashcards and worksheets. It seems the adults don't realize that the first and most engaging encounter many children have with two-dimensional shapes is as the *faces* of building blocks as well as of many objects in the world around them. Activities like Mr. Barry's *Tower Challenge* bring the relationship between two- and three-dimensional shapes to life.

The tally sheet that Emerson and the other children worked on quickly extends into another phase of the children's inquiry about shapes. Not surprisingly, the blocks most used to build the towers are rectangular prisms and cubes, with cylinders a close third. Pyramids and hemispheres are used only at the top of the structures. Throughout, the children are more likely to refer to these solids as *blocks* (rectangular prisms), *ramps* (triangular prisms), and **towers** or pillars (cylinders). The children learn about the defining attributes through their hands and eyes; the labels become both meaningful and useful ways to describe their thinking and problem solving when it comes to explaining why the six *flat faces* of **rectangular prisms** are most versatile for building while the *rounded sides* of **cylinders** limit the way they can be oriented. In the same way **triangular prisms** (of whose five faces, three are rectangles and two are triangles) make good ramps.

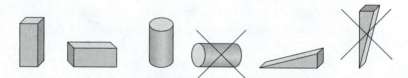

Flat Faces of Shapes Are Most Versatile for Building

Pre-K and kindergarten children alike can solidify their understanding of the attributes of shapes by developing lists of things in the world around us that are *boxes*, *cans*, or that are shaped like triangles or circles. They are also ready for rich conversations about why some things are made in one shape or why another shape might be used in a different situation.

Focusing on the attributes rather than terminology in the way that Mr. Barry does avoids the all-too-common practice of teaching vocabulary, with the assumption that being able to use technical names is the same as understanding. As we have said, it is much more important that young children use their eyes and hands to make sense of the defining attributes of shapes. They can trace around both

Math Snapshot

Mr. Barry set out a number of cardboard boxes at the art table. During center time, he sat there and patiently took several boxes apart along the glued edges, showing the children how they could refold the flattened cardboard to make the 3D box again, using tape. With large pieces of construction paper, several kids started making their own boxes based on the flattened cardboard patterns. Mr. Barry explained that the flat version is called a *net*.

He knew the children were beginning to see the relationships between three-dimensional solids and two-dimensional shapes when Gabriel made the connection between these "nets" and the classroom set of colorful shape tiles whose edges are magnetized to make it easy to make 3D shapes. He was very serious as he told Mr. Barry, "If you are doing a tricky shape like a pyramid, you should use magnet tiles because they will just 'SNAP' but the tape always makes the boxes kind of squished."

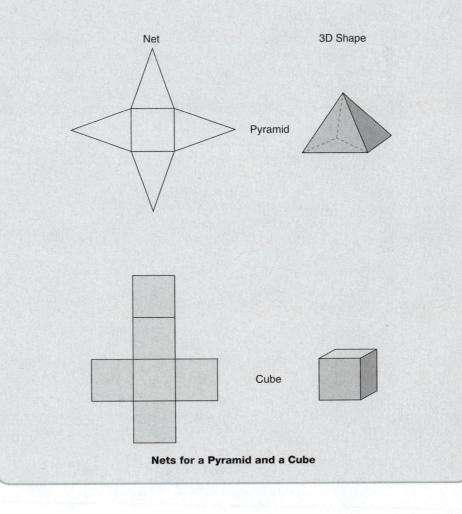

Nets for a Pyramid and a Cube

the two- and three-dimensional shapes so that they can literally feel how the lines can be curved or straight. Gestures can also help emphasize that the straight lines of two-dimensional shapes always are joined at points we commonly call *corners*. Shapes with curved lines, such as circles and ovals, are also joined but one thing that makes them distinct from the shapes mathematically known as **polygons** is that they do not have corners. The important point is that the children need to have a strong foundational awareness that there is a close connection between the shapes we see on paper and the shapes of objects in the world.

Big Idea: Shapes Can Be Combined and Separated (Composed and Decomposed) to Make New Shapes

Math Snapshot

Mr. Barry introduces a new activity—he puts the stamps, a variety of stickers of shapes in different sizes and colors, and some shape templates in the art corner and invites the children to work on creating pictures out of shapes. He suggests that some might want to see what happens if they only use one shape—such as all kinds of circles in different sizes or colors. Or they might want to use a variety of shapes to show a creature, such as those found in two beloved books, *Color Zoo* by Lois Ehlert, and *Whoo, Whoo* by David Carter.

Carlie looks with satisfaction at her picture of a Princess Cat. "I used lots of triangles," she says proudly. "I just matched two triangles together to make diamonds for the crown!!"

Child's Art of "Princess Cat"

Having children make pictures using shapes engages them in exploring how rotating, combining, and changing size can produce very different effects. They can build on their understanding of how two- and three-dimensional shapes are related to see the many important relationships that are within and between shapes. This will prepare them to discover another important Big Idea: Many shapes can be made up of or broken down into other shapes.

Knowing that a rhombus (commonly called a diamond) can be formed by two equilateral triangles and that two right triangles form a rectangle reinforces the defining attributes of each shape. At the same time, it lays useful groundwork for complicated mathematical ideas such as *fractions* and *area*. Young children aren't developmentally ready for these concepts in any detail. However, making shape pictures and playing with pattern blocks, tangrams, and unit blocks lays an important foundation. It also gives the children the satisfaction and joy of making these discoveries for themselves—as Carlie did with her princess cat.

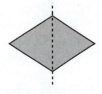

Triangles That Make a Rhombus and a Rectangle

Math Snapshot

Throughout the school year, Mr. Barry regularly includes shape puzzles as a math center choice. Early in the year, he used pattern block worksheets that included guidelines to show which specific blocks to use to fill each form. Children laid the blocks directly on top to complete each puzzle. He soon realized that many of the children found these models not only too easy but also too limiting. By the end of six weeks, most children chose to use the cardboard templates that provided an outline of a form that could be filled using a variety of different combinations of the blocks.

Different Types of Pattern-Block Puzzles

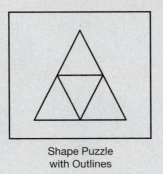

Shape Puzzle
with Outlines

Open Shape
Template

(continued)

As the Morning Math challenge one day, Mr. Barry announces a "Make This Star Your Own" Challenge. He puts out 10 cutout outlines of a 6-pointed star, a large supply of pattern blocks, and several small trays on a table in the math corner. Throughout the morning the children work to see how many different combinations of pattern blocks they can use to fill the frame. When the group comes together just before lunch, Mr. Barry puts out six small trays showing completely different solutions and asks what children notice.

Ella points out that two of the six designs use only one shape: one features 12 green triangles, the other uses 6 blue rhomboids. Mr. Barry moves those two trays next to each other and wonders if anyone has any idea why this works. "I know! If you put two green triangles together in the right way, it's the same as the blue one," Pete announces. He is happy to demonstrate using some of the spare blocks. "Hey, it's like doubles," Emerson exclaims. "Six and six is twelve."

Mr. Barry gives thumbs up to Emerson's comment but wonders if anyone has any other discoveries. "Three of the patterns use the six green triangles for the pointy parts of the star," Henry notes.

"And this is the only one that doesn't use any green triangles!" Tyrone adds, pointing to six blue rhomboids.

Ava and Ellie are eager to point out that they came up with a solution that used one red trapezoid, two blue rhomboids, and four green triangles. "Ours is the trickiest!" they declare.

Davita disagrees, "But it doesn't even look like a star with all those colors. When we did all the triangles, we used 12—that's the most pieces. You only have seven!"

"Actually," Mr. Barry says, "It looks to me as if everyone has really had their thinking caps on this morning! Tomorrow I'm going to bring photos and a chart to our meeting showing the six different ways you found to make this star."

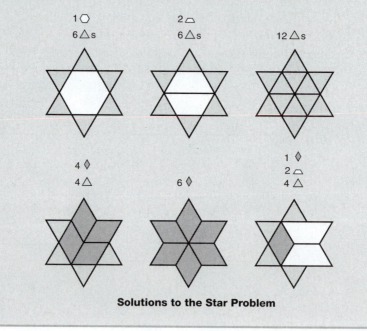

Solutions to the Star Problem

Mr. Barry intentionally chose pattern blocks for this activity because he knows the six shapes included in the standard set bear specific relationships to each other. The fact that they are color coded gives children a way to identify them as having precise attributes without having to know the technical name. At the same time, the colors make the many different solutions highly visible and easy to discuss. Finally, many of the solution designs show a line of symmetry—an important mathematical attribute that most regular shapes have.

When Mr. Barry brings the chart showing the six solutions the children found to the group, he will use questions to help the children "unpack" or develop their understanding of the defining characteristics as well as of the relationships between two-dimensional shapes. Thus when the group discusses the question, *Which of the six ways work by changing the yellow hexagon into other shapes?* the children are excited to see that there are "rules" they can use when changing a design. Any time they have used a hexagon, they could put in two red trapezoids or three blue rhomboids or six green (equilateral) triangles.

In the course of the discussion, Emerson is very excited by a new discovery; he sees that since green triangles can be substituted for both the red trapezoid and the blue rhomboid, there is another way to make the star. He quickly shifts Avi and Ellie's one blue rhombus into two triangles and announces triumphantly, "Look, now this one has eight pieces instead of seven. Plus, now it can be split in half with that simtree line!"

A few are not sure what Emerson means, but soon catch on as others in the group point out how the other designs also can be split so that the two sides are exactly mirror images of each other.

Awareness of *mirror symmetry* as a mathematical property often doesn't make sense until children are in kindergarten. However, when they reach this developmental point, children's drawings and designs show symmetry—whether or not they are familiar with the term. Teachers like Mr. Barry, who are tuned into the way mathematics is all around us, can use comments like Emerson's to mathematize concepts like symmetry and to deepen their exploration of the intricate relationships between regular shapes.

Implications for Teaching

While it is clear that topics involving numbers deserve several chapters, the reasons for devoting two chapters to geometry may seem less clear. In a sense, our decision was driven by the way that this major content area of mathematics is so often relegated to the back burner until children are solidly into middle childhood. But by then, they are quickly called upon to grapple with measuring specific aspects of regular shapes, whether the area, perimeter, and circumference of a rectangle or circle, or the angles of a triangle. They will also be called upon to use the rules of geometry (for example, that all the interior angles of a rectangle measure 90 degrees) to build logical arguments, called proofs. Relying on the rules that govern how we define shapes, these proofs ask children to combine the many different known facts to demonstrate new truths. All of these activities, however, seem firmly in the realm of school mathematics, with little relevance to real life.

One of the central concerns of this book is that school mathematics is sometimes seen as tiresome, irrelevant, and demanding, precisely because little is done to alert young children to the many ways it connects to our everyday lives. The world young children experience is filled with interesting and important mathematical features and problem situations, but many of these are not apparent to them without adult guidance.

Geometry is a striking case in point. In the previous chapter on spatial relationships, we saw how central to daily life issues of spatial relationships are, and how mathematical attributes create precision in our descriptions of and plans for both movement and location. Our glimpse into Mr. Barry's classroom in this chapter is meant to build on those ideas, illustrating how the idea of "shape" is a means to define some specific types of spaces, which allows us to be increasingly precise about how they work. Mr. Barry offered opportunities for children to see that shapes—both two- and three-dimensional—are defined by rules, that two-dimensional shapes can be found as the faces of three-dimensional shapes, and that shapes can be combined and separated to make new shapes. As you think about how to address these Big Ideas of Shape in your classroom, we hope you will keep in mind the following implications for your teaching.

Provide a Diversity of Shape Examples

One of the classic mistakes educators of young children make when working with shapes is to present only highly typical, stereotyped versions of each shape. That is, all rectangles are shaped like doors, all triangles have three equal sides and rest on a base, and so on. Young children will benefit greatly from seeing long, skinny rectangles and short, fat rectangles alongside rectangles that are also squares. Triangles are a particularly diverse group of shapes, and children need to see right triangles, isosceles triangles (two sides the same length) and scalene triangles (three angles all different sizes), and they need to see them rotated so that sometimes they rest on a point as opposed to a flat base. Only when there are different examples of the same shape will children have enough information to deduce the rules that govern that shape.

The same is true of three-dimensional shapes. Do an inventory of your block corner: you may be surprised to find that rectangular prisms are well-represented, but little else is there. Some of you will have pillars (cylinders) and ramps (triangular prisms), but pyramids and spheres are likely lacking. There are sets widely available for purchase of three-dimensional solids in which these shapes are well-represented, some made of wood and others of foam. The magnet tiles Gabriel referred to in an earlier "teacher talk" provide an option so that children can construct at least some three-dimensional shapes themselves. As with two-dimensional shapes, the ideal is to present several different versions of each three-dimensional shape so that children will be prompted to think about the key qualities they have in common. Certainly that will be possible to do for rectangular prisms if you have a good-sized set of unit blocks, but you may have to work harder to include many other three-dimensional shapes.

Move Children toward Precision

When children get excited about seeing a shape, they often have a tendency to overgeneralize, seeing slices of pizza as triangles or flower pots as cylinders. While it's important to embrace children's enthusiasm and keep them engaged, it is also important to provide the information they need to get their shape definitions as "right" as possible. Don't let these moments go; respond by acknowledging that you understand their idea, and then help them see where the details diverge, as in *"You're right, Yolanda, that yield sign does look like a triangle, except it doesn't have pointy corners, does it?"* If you are ready and willing to talk about shapes with lots of specificity and precision, children will begin to attempt to do so, too.

Finally, be sure that children have opportunities to work with "nonexamples." The circle with a gap in its circumference, the wedge-shape with one curved edge that is not really a triangle, and the quadrilateral whose corners are not square can be a source of rich discussion. Talk that includes questions such as "What makes it *like* a circle? Why is it *not* a circle? What would we have to do to *make* it a circle?" is just right for helping children see the attributes of shapes and become analytical about them.

Development of Ideas about Shape

There is a wide range of thinking about shapes among children between the ages of 3 and 6, and just as in other math topics, their thinking may be quite advanced in one area and surprisingly simplistic in another. An idea that makes sense in the block corner may not work anymore at the art center, and vice versa. Regardless, Table 9.1 describes the things children may do in your classroom related to each of the Big Ideas as their thinking about shapes develops. We hope this will help you observe and understand their behavior, and decide what kinds of experiences are best to support progress in their understanding of shapes.

TABLE 9.1   How Thinking about Shapes Develops

Big Idea	Emerging	Developing	Proficient	Activities
Shapes can be defined and classified by their attributes.	• Uses names of 2D shapes as labels, with no clear association to attributes • May confuse shapes of the same type based on orientation or size ("an upside-down triangle") • May be "fooled" by size or color of shapes	• Beginning awareness of attributes, as in "triangles have 3 sides" • May be "fooled" by some non-examples ("a slice of pizza is a triangle") • No longer fooled by size or color	• Able to apply attribute rules to unusual shape examples—knows that an acute triangle is still a triangle • Able to ignore unusual orientations—can see that a square standing on its corner is still a square	• "Mystery Bag" games with 2D and 3D shapes. For 2D, use cardstock or thin plastic shapes • Shape "I Spy" games • Shape scavenger hunts
The flat faces of 3-dimensional shapes are 2-dimensional shapes.	Uses only every-day language to describe 3D solids, such as "ball" and "block"	Uses names of 2D shapes to describe 3D shapes—a unit block is a "rectangle"	Sees and can describe the faces on a 3D solid—a rectangular prism has 6 rectangle-shaped sides	• Use 3D solids with washable paint to make "prints" of faces • Impress 3D solids in play dough • Construct 3D solids out of play dough • Make pyramids and prisms with magnet tiles
Shapes can be combined and separated (composed and decomposed) to make new shapes.	Begins to see shape combinations in the world—"a house is a square with a triangle for the roof"	Can solve simple jigsaw-type puzzles that require children to attend to the shape (and not just the picture) of the pieces	Can combine and substitute shapes systematically, as in 2 right triangles put together to make a square	• Pattern block puzzles and frames • Tangram puzzles • Geoboards

The activities suggested in this chart get the Big Ideas into children's eyes, ears, hands, and feet by giving them opportunities to explore and define shapes that are so much a part of the world all around us. Learning shapes names is not the emphasis for young children; they do not necessarily need to be introduced to the more technical mathematical terms in the "shape primer" in Table 9.2. Instead, we adults should be looking for evidence that they *see* the attributes that differentiate types of shapes, and helping them find vocabulary to describe these differences when they ask for it.

Basic Shape Categories

Some types of shapes—such as triangles or quadrilaterals—can be broken down into increasingly specific categories with their own particular rules. Each row of our table takes a broad shape type, defines it, and then moves on to identify the specific categories within it. You will see that we give special attention to shapes children see most often, and sometimes provide both common and technical shape names. As the columns move to the right, the shapes become less common and more unusual.

The first few rows of Table 9.2 focuses on two-dimensional shapes—those that we draw on paper or see as the side of a box or the face of a clock. Three-dimensional shapes like cubes and spheres follow.

TABLE 9.2   Shape Primer

TWO DIMENSIONAL SHAPES		
Polygons • Shape is closed (no gaps) • Must have at least 3 sides • All sides are straight		
Basic Shape Category	**Most Common Types**	**Less Common Types**
Triangles • 3 straight sides • 3 corners/angles • Angles add to 180 degrees	**Equilateral triangle** • 3 sides of equal length • 3 angles of equal size	**Isosceles triangle** • 2 sides of equal length • 2 angles of equal size
 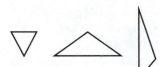		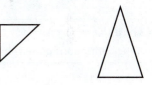
	Right triangle • 1 square corner (or "right" angle) • 2 pointed (acute) angles	**Other triangles** • Named by type of angles (acute or obtuse) or length of sides (scalene)
	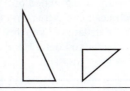	

(*Continued*)

TABLE 9.2   Shape Primer   (*Continued*)

Basic Shape Category	Most Common Types	Less Common Types

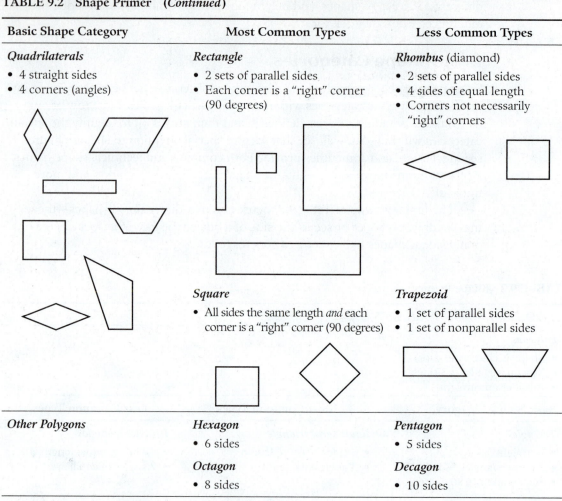

Quadrilaterals
- 4 straight sides
- 4 corners (angles)

Rectangle
- 2 sets of parallel sides
- Each corner is a "right" corner (90 degrees)

Rhombus (diamond)
- 2 sets of parallel sides
- 4 sides of equal length
- Corners not necessarily "right" corners

Square
- All sides the same length *and* each corner is a "right" corner (90 degrees)

Trapezoid
- 1 set of parallel sides
- 1 set of nonparallel sides

Other Polygons

Hexagon
- 6 sides

Octagon
- 8 sides

Pentagon
- 5 sides

Decagon
- 10 sides

Curved shapes (*not polygons*)
- One continuous closed shape containing a curve

Circle
- All points are the same distance from center

Oval
- Friendly: A "stretched out" circle!
- Technical: Has 2 foci, and the sum of distances from any point on its edge to Focus 1 and Focus 2 is always the same

Semi-Circle
- One curved line
- One straight line
- Half a circle

(*Continued*)

THREE-DIMENSIONAL SHAPES

Polyhedron
- All faces are flat
- All edges are straight

Basic Shape Category	Most Common Types	Less Common Types
Prism • Bases: 2 parallel faces are same shape and size w/no curved edges (congruent polygons) • Lateral faces: 3 or more flat faces are rectangles (or other parallelograms) that connect the bases to one another along congruent edges	**Rectangular prism** • Bases are rectangles **Cube** • Bases are square *and* lateral faces are square 	**Triangular prism** • Bases are triangles 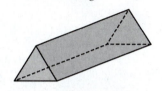 **Other prisms** • Named by shape of 2 bases (pentagonal prism, for example) 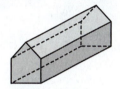
Pyramid • 1 base • 3 or more triangular lateral faces meet at the top (the apex)	**Square pyramid** • Base is a square 	**Triangular pyramid** • Base is a triangle **Other pyramids** • Named by the shape of the base (hexagonal pyramid, for example)

(*Continued*)

TABLE 9.2   Shape Primer   (*Continued*)

Basic Shape Category	Most Common Types	Less Common Types

Solids with curves (*not polyhedrons*)

Sphere

- No flat faces, no edges or vertices
- Shaped like a ball
- All points on the surface of a sphere are the same distance from its center

Cylinder

- 2 flat circle-shaped bases, parallel to one another
- 1 curved side connecting the bases to one another

Hemisphere

- 1 curved surface
- 1 flat circle-shaped face
- Shaped like half a sphere

Ovoid (egg)

- No flat faces, no edges or vertices
- Shaped like an egg

Cone

- 1 flat, circle-shaped base
- 1 curved side
- 1 apex (point at top)

Finding Great Math in Great Books

There are many wonderful books that alert us all—including adults—to the way that shapes are all around us.

- Tana Hoban's beautiful photographic concept books such as *Shapes, Shapes, Shapes* and *I Read Signs* invite discovery and discussion from the youngest children.
- *When a Line Bends . . . A Shape Begins* by Rhonda Greene is a playful introduction that shapes and lines are very closely related. *Mouse Shapes* by Ellen Stoll Walsh is equally delightful in inviting thinking about shapes.
- *Round Is a Mooncake: A Book of Shapes* by Roseanne Thong and Grace Lin is just one of many books that focus on attributes of specific shapes. The story celebrates how circles are important in Chinese culture.
- Thanks to technology, amazing things can be done with mass produced die-cuts and pop-ups such as Lois Ehlert's *Color Farm* and *Color Zoo*. *Whoo? Whoo?* and *Woof Woof* by David Carter are two other examples.
- *Grandfather Tang's Story* by Ann Tompert has deservedly become a classic mathematical tale. Children from 5 to 8—if not 18 or 81—can relate to this tale of how the desire to be the *strongest* can tempt us to forget that the most important strength requires us to not hurt others. *Tangram Tales* by Diane De Las Casas provides a whole series of stories that use tangrams.

Video Link

As you watch the video *Feel For Shapes*, here are some points to reflect on.

1. What are ways that the teacher clearly puts the emphasis on the defining attributes of shapes instead of on the name alone?

2. The children in the video are young preschoolers; what are ways this activity might look different in a kindergarten classroom like Mr. Barry's?

3. What evidence do you see that children are engaged and are actively constructing their own understanding?

Conclusion

The focus on **Big Ideas** throughout this book reflects our belief that teachers play a central and crucial role in helping young children build a strong foundation in mathematics. And, we know that teachers are more successful when they use the Big Ideas to guide their activity planning, classroom conversations, and responses to children's many questions. Accomplishing this requires two essential components:

- Teaching that is both intentional and reflective; and
- A coherent, deep, integrated understanding of math content for young children.

 ## Intentional Teaching and Reflection

As we hope this text acknowledges, good early childhood teaching is an art. In order to maintain a safe and pleasant classroom that young children will want to be in, the early childhood teacher must pay a great deal of attention to—and be willing to adjust to—individual differences among children. He or she must pay ample attention to children's physical health and comfort, to their feelings, and to their developing (though sometimes primitive!) social skills. The effective management of these aspects of children's functioning is a baseline requirement for learning of any kind to take place. While the best teachers of older children also pay attention to these kinds of concerns, they do not occupy the same amount of space and time in their teaching.

Because of these considerations, it is especially challenging to address content, such as mathematics, in early childhood classrooms. Linking the new to the known is harder when students bring very little knowledge and experience. To do so, early childhood teachers must find ways to connect important content to children's existing interests, skills, and understanding—an opportunistic type of teaching that requires close observation of children and a flexible, accommodating approach to pedagogy. If such teaching is to be not only responsive to children but also guide them to think about new content, the teacher must hold a solid sense of appropriate learning goals firmly in mind.

When teachers are tuned in to children's mathematical understanding, they can plan and introduce activities that specifically address children's mathematical development and that have specific learning goals. In other words, effective teaching is intentional; it calls for using formative assessment to determine where children are in relation to learning goals and to provide the right kind and amount of support for them to continue to make progress—as NAEYC (National Association of the Education of Young Children) has long held as a principle.

In the story above, Tracy is wise to recognize that the support of her colleagues will bolster her attempts to change her practice. Talking about teaching with other teachers can keep you focused on those parts of teaching you can control—your own actions—and give you encouragement and ideas when you feel discouraged. Hearing how things went in another classroom can provide a new vision for what is possible, and making plans with others is a good way to hold yourself accountable for trying something new. We don't all have the luxury of working with colleagues to improve our teaching, but some form of explicit planning and reflection—even if it is in a journal—will make a huge difference in how intentional you can be.

A Connected Vision of the Big Ideas of Early Mathematics

Math Snapshot

During her weekly book group, Tracy tells her colleagues how having the Big Ideas in the back of her mind helps her feel more prepared to respond to her children's thinking.

She gives the example of Sam, who said off-handedly to her one day at snack time, "My oranges are a square." Tracy admits that in the past, she would have likely let a random comment like that go. This time, however, she asked Sam to tell her more. "See, there's four," he explained as he gestured to the arrangement of his orange slices on his napkin.

"So, Sam is connecting his knowledge about shapes with the number 4. Not such a random comment after all!" laughs Tracy.

Because we are talking about early childhood teaching, intentional teachers help children explore mathematical questions throughout the day and across various contexts—whole group, small group, centers, play, and routines. This is a demanding role for teachers—to carefully observe children, accurately interpret their mathematical development, and plan and implement appropriate activities to further their learning—and it requires a deep, connected understanding of the Big Ideas.

Having a deep understanding of the Big Ideas enables us to recognize the mathematics that children are ready to learn as well as how they may be thinking. It equips us to offer feedback that helps children see the math underlying the situation by noticing (*"I see how you . . ."*), by asking (*"What do you think will happen if . . .? How do you know?"*), and by modeling (*"Look what happens when I . . ."*).

Although we have presented the Big Ideas through a series of nine chapters, organized by topic, we believe it is essential that every early childhood teacher notice and understand connections between and among the ideas. It is all "mathematics," after all. Dividing it into different topics makes it easier to write about, but we find that, no matter what we do, there are lots of ideas that seem to belong in several different places at the same time!

Rather than seeing this fact as a problem, we see it as one of the more fascinating qualities of this body of knowledge: connections between ideas of measurement and geometry (for example) can provide insights that inform our sense of number and even influence how we think about data. We hope that, as you have become more familiar with the Big Ideas, you have begun to notice concepts and terms that crop up again and again, and have begun to think about why that is so.

Just to kick start your thinking about these "cross-topic" connections between mathematical ideas, we briefly discuss five terms that seem to have many different kinds of mathematical homes: attribute, unit, composition and decomposition, comparison, and structure.

- **Attribute.** *Recognizing and defining attributes* is important for making sets to count and compare. The first requirement of measuring is deciding *what attribute to measure*—what kind of "big" are we talking about. Then, children learn to compare and quantify *how much of an attribute* an object possesses (length, for example). In order to classify geometric shapes, young children need to learn to *recognize the attributes of shapes*, not simply to learn to name them. This is because the name carries with it the particular attributes of the shape. In all contexts, the development in early childhood is towards *increasingly precise description of attributes*.

- **Unit.** In order to extend or create a repeating pattern, children must identify the *unit that repeats*. To measure length, children select a *unit length measure*: block lengths or inches, for example. When children count, they must create *mental units* of what they are going to count: shoes or pairs of shoes, for example. And eventually, children begin to understand how our base-10 number system relies on grouping by tens to make *new units*.

- **Composition and Decomposition.** When children recognize the quantity of a set, they often view the set as *composed of two or more smaller quantities* that they can subitize. A flexible number sense relies on children knowing how to *decompose numbers from 1 to 10* into all possible pairs. For numbers from 11 to 19, they must understand how to *compose teen numbers* with a 10 and some 1s. *Composing and decomposing sets* is the basis of joining and separating situations and other number operations. In geometry, children often view shapes as *composed of other shapes*. For example, two trapezoids compose a hexagon.

- **Comparison.** As soon as children are able to examine two pictures, objects, or ideas and hold them both in their mind, they naturally *compare* to decide which is more and which is less. They *compare and order* objects by size (as in measurement) and sets of objects by quantity (as when counting). By *comparing*, they come to see equality and inequality in many different types of number and measurement contexts. Because mathematical thinking is always relational thinking, *comparison* processes run throughout.

- **Structure.** When children see patterns and organize information, they take steps toward recognizing the *structure of mathematics*. Throughout mathematics, *structure* can be found in number, shapes, and space. The search for patterns and *structure* connects all mathematical thinking; and when we find *structure*, it allows us to make generalizations and solve problems.

Such connections are not merely interesting—in many cases, they are crucial to basic mathematical understanding. For example, the coordination of subitizing, counting, and an understanding of cardinality connects many Big Ideas and is the best route to a meaningful understanding of the number system. These kinds of overarching concepts connect mathematical ideas, procedures, and problem situations into a unified body of knowledge. They portray mathematics as a coherent and sense-making endeavor. If mathematics is an integrated body of knowledge for you, with many meaningful connections among its ideas, you stand a much better chance of helping the children in your care see it that way.

Implications for Teaching

Technically, we've reached the conclusion of our discussion of Big Ideas in early mathematics. But, as we said in the opening of this chapter, the rewarding and challenging work of reflective practice never ends. Even though you have persevered this far, it is likely you still have questions about the Big Ideas as well as about how to teach them more effectively. One of the rewards of being part of the Early Math Collaborative is that our own understanding of both those points is constantly being deepened—and our questions keep multiplying. In the spirit of this kind of ongoing exploration, we'd like to suggest it might be best not to put this book on a shelf, but instead, to dip into it again and again.

- Perhaps there is a topic that you want to review?

- Maybe you have a colleague or two who would join you in doing a lesson study of one of the activities described in the math snapshots?

- Would a discussion of one of the video clips be a productive way to spend a team meeting?

- Could you draft a lesson plan to emphasize the ideas in one chapter and then sit down to review and improve the plan after trying it out?

Whatever you do or don't do with the text, please be sure to keep calling on the Big Ideas as you support young children in exploring and mathematizing all the wonders of the world around us.

 Finding Great Math in Great Books

There are other great resources to help you continue to grow as a professional. The titles below are ones that have influenced our work, and we are sure that you will find them helpful, too.

- For more activity ideas, look to *Developing Math Concepts in Pre-Kindergarten* by Kathy Richardson. Sally Moomaw's *More Than Counting: Math Activities for Preschool and Kindergarten, Standard Edition* provides lesson plans and games that use a problem-solving approach.

- There are several excellent books on block play that are well worth having on hand to stimulate your ideas about how to make this kind of play meaningful. They include *Building Structures with Young Children* by Ingrid Chalufour; *Teaching Numeracy, Language, and Literacy with Blocks* by Abigail Neuberger and Elizabeth Vaughn; and *Block Play* by Sharon McDonald.

- A great children's book is a great way to spark mathematical conversations. *Math and Literature, Grades K–1* by Marilyn Burns and Stephanie Sheffield provides specific examples of how to use quality literature to build mathematical understanding. *Cowboys Count, Monkeys Measure, & Princesses Problem Solve: Building Early Math Skills Through Storybooks* by Jane M. Wilburne, Jane B. Keat, and Mary Napoli is also excellent and targets pre-K–third grade.

- *Supporting Language Learners in Math Class: Grades K–2* by Rusty Bresser, K. Melanese, and C. Sphaar is a valuable discussion of how to use second language learning strategies, such as sentence frames, to develop mathematical understanding.

- For more information on research about early math teaching and learning, see the bibliography at the end of this book for recommended resources.

Big Ideas Charts

Sets

Number Sense

Counting

Number Operations

Pattern

Measurement

Data Analysis

Spatial Relationships

Shape

Big Ideas of Sets

Topic	Big Ideas	Examples
Sets and Sorting	• Attributes can be used to sort collections into sets.	• Color, size, shape, type of object, etc.
	• The same collection can be sorted in different ways.	• Red bears vs. blue bears; big bears vs. little bears
	• Sets can be compared and ordered.	• *There are more red bears than blue bears.* (compare); *small bears, medium bears, large bears* (order)

Big Ideas of Number Sense

Topic	Big Ideas	Examples
Uses of Number ⭐⭐⭐⭐⭐ (circled, arrow pointing to last star) 5th	• Numbers are used many ways, some more mathematical than others.	• *Tommy has 5 books.* (cardinal) • *Ava is fifth in line today.* (ordinal) • Numbers on basketball jerseys, home addresses, telephone numbers (nominal) • *Let's meet at 5 p.m. on December 5.* (referential)
Numerosity ⭐⭐⭐⭐⭐ = 5	• Quantity is an attribute of a set of objects, and we use numbers to name specific quantities. • The quantity of a small collection can be intuitively perceived without counting.	• 5 mice and 5 elephants are alike in quantity, though different in other ways. • Children just "see" three objects and know it's 3.

Big Ideas of Counting

Topic	Big Ideas	Examples
Quantity "1, 2, 3, 4, 5 . . . 5!"	• Counting can be used to find out "how many" in a collection.	• *1, 2, 3, 4, 5, 6 . . . you used six blocks!*
Counting Rules	• Counting has rules that apply to any collection.	• "One, four, two" doesn't give a correct answer. *(stable order)* • Children need strategies for keeping track, like touch-pointing or moving to another pile. *(one-to-one correspondence)* • Mixing up objects and counting again is a good exercise; the third object counted is not the only one that can "be" three *(order irrelevance)* • Being able to count is not the same as being able to answer "how many?" *(cardinality)*

Big Ideas of Number Operations

Topic	Big Ideas	Examples
Changing Sets ☆☆ + ☆☆☆	• Sets can be *changed* by adding items (joining) or by taking some away (separating).	• *You have 2 balls and I have 3 balls. How many balls do we have altogether?* • *You had 12 cards, and you gave your friend 5. How many do you have now?*
Comparing Sets ☆☆ < ☆☆☆	• Sets can be *compared* using the attribute of numerosity, and *ordered* by more than, less than, and equal to.	• *I have a handful of raisins; Chris has a bowlful. Chris has more!* • *I have 1 pear and 1 peach; you have 2 apples. We have the same number of fruits.* • *Avery has 3 dirty plates, and Tracy has 4 dirty bowls. Who has fewer dishes to wash?*
Number Composition (★★★) (★★)	• A quantity (whole) can be *decomposed* into equal or unequal parts; the parts can be *composed* to form the whole.	• *How many ways can you show 5 with fingers on both hands?*

Big Ideas of Pattern

Topic	Big Ideas	Examples
Pattern and Regularity	• Patterns are sequences (repeating or growing) governed by a rule; they exist both in the world and in mathematics.	• Dots on a ladybug; posts of a fence; adding 1 to any number gives you the next number.
	• Identifying the rule of a pattern brings predictability and allows us to make generalizations.	• *After lunch comes recess; If we keep counting people's feet, it will always be 2 more.*
	• The same pattern can be found in many different forms.	• Big block, little block; big block little block; big block, little block . . . OR snap, clap; snap, clap; snap, clap . . .

Big Ideas of Measurement

Topic	Big Ideas	Examples
Attributes	• Many different attributes can be measured, even when measuring a single object.	• A bucket has many measurable attributes, including height, weight, capacity, or circumference: *What kind of "big" is it?*
Comparison	• All measurement involves a "fair" comparison.	• Weighing rocks on a pan balance (direct comparison); using a length of string to measure a table in one room and chairs in another (indirect comparison). • A "fair" comparison measures the same attribute. Units must be of equal size, with no gaps or overlaps.
Precision	• Quantifying a measurement helps us describe and compare more precisely.	• Nonstandard units (such as blocks) and standard units (such as inches) allow for more precision than direct comparison. • There is always a more precise measurement possible—we never get it exactly "right," but it must be "good enough" for the task at hand.

Big Ideas of Data Analysis

Topic	Big Ideas	Examples
Gathering Data *What kind of pets does our class have?*	• The purpose of collecting data is to answer questions when the answers are not immediately obvious.	• Children's own questions are most meaningful to them; often the need to gather data will come naturally in the course of discussion or from content areas such as science and social studies.
Organizing Data Hamsters | Cats | Fish | Dogs	• Data must be represented in order to be interpreted, and how data are gathered and organized depends on the question.	• Age-appropriate data collection methods: sort real objects; organize pictures, counters, or name cards; make tallies; survey friends or family. • A tally chart can help with seeing clusters in the data; a bar graph provides an easy way to compare quantities across categories.
Describing Data	• It is useful to compare parts of the data and to draw conclusions about the data as a whole.	• *There are more dogs than fish. But overall, hamsters are the most common pet.*

Big Ideas of Spatial Relationships

Topic	Big Ideas	Examples
Describing Space	• Relationships between objects and places can be described with mathematical precision.	• Maps and models represent the three-dimensional world. • *Joshua is in front of Ana, and he is behind Tameika.*
Visualizing Space	• Our own experiences of space and two-dimensional representations of space reflect a specific point of view. • Spatial relationships can be visualized and manipulated mentally.	• A party hat looks triangular from the side, but when you lay it down, it can look like a circle. • An expert jigsaw-puzzle solver can picture a missing piece and does not rely on trial and error.

Big Ideas of Shape

Topic	Big Ideas	Examples
Defining and Analyzing Shapes	• Shapes can be defined and classified by their attributes. • The flat faces of solid (three-dimensional) shapes are two-dimensional shapes. • Shapes can be combined and separated (composed and decomposed) to make new shapes.	• A rectangle must have two sets of parallel sides of equal length and four 90° angles; thus, a square is a special type of rectangle. • A baseball is a sphere and can be represented in a drawing as a circle. • Any rectangle can be divided into 2 triangles.

© Erikson Institute's Early Math Collaborative. Reprinted from *Big Ideas of Early Mathematics* (2014), Pearson Education.

Book Study Guide
for
Big Ideas of Early Mathematics: What Teachers of Young Children Need to Know

Consider reading and discussing this book as part of a *professional learning community* (PLC) at your center or school. A PLC is a collaborative structure in which groups of teachers and administrators seek and share learning and then act on what they learn. The goal is to become more effective as professionals so that children benefit.

The following questions are provided to provoke discussion. We hope they will be just the beginning of your collegial conversations about early mathematics!

Introduction

1. Tracy, the teacher described in the book's opening, is a good teacher who feels less than confident about her math teaching. To what extent do you identify with her? What has influenced your own attitudes and beliefs about mathematics?

2. Big Ideas are key concepts that lay the foundation for lifelong mathematical learning and thinking. What Big Ideas do you already emphasize in your math teaching?

3. What does the term *mathematize* mean to you? Describe a time when you helped children recognize the math concepts inherent in their play or daily activities.

4. Why do you think the authors emphasize the importance of *receptive understanding*? How can you assess receptive understanding—what are possible sources of evidence?

5. After reading about the format of this book, how do you plan to use it? Will you read all the chapters in order? Are there particular topics you'd like to read first? Define your own purposes for reading this book.

Chapter 1: Sets
Using Attributes to Make Collections

1. Sorting activities are commonplace in preschool and Kindergarten. Have you ever thought of sorting as *math*? How might you explain to a parent that sorting is "doing math"?

2. The Math Snapshots in this chapter describe how Ms. Simone integrates math into her center time and her whole-group time. Where do you find time for math in your classroom?

3. Look at the chart of activities for exploring sets (Table 1.1). What kind of activities do you see yourself using? Why?

4. Make a list of materials you have available for sorting activities. Are you satisfied with the range and quality of items? What materials might you add or replace?

5. Modify a sorting activity you have used in the past or create a new lesson that focuses on the Big Ideas of Sets. Explain your instructional decisions.

Chapter 2: Number Sense
Developing a Meaningful Sense of Quantity

1. *Number sense* can mean many different things to different people. Read the authors's definition. How close is that definition to your own?

2. Describe the mathematical ability called *subitizing*. The authors claim that subitizing is an innate ability. Do you believe this to be true based on your experiences with young children? Provide specific examples.

3. What teaching strategies from this chapter—start with small numbers; link numbers to objects, actions, ideas, and symbols; address visual number sense; and, build a sense of magnitude—do you see yourself using? Why?

4. Have you developed a lesson or strategy you use with children that you think improves number sense? Describe why it is effective.

5. After reading this chapter, how would you rate the importance of number sense for early mathematics? Is this the same as you felt before reading the chapter or has your thinking changed?

Chapter 3: Counting
More Than Just 1, 2, 3

1. The principle of cardinality is the cornerstone of competent counting. In what ways do children demonstrate an understanding of cardinality—what does it look like?

2. Make a list of opportunities for authentic reasons for children to count during a typical day in your classroom. If you haven't previously tried them all, select one or two new ways to involve children in counting with a purpose.

3. Look at the chart of activities to support the counting principles (Table 3.1). What kinds of activities do you see yourself using? Why?

4. What is your favorite counting book? In your opinion, what makes it particularly effective?

5. Consider how counting is assessed and reported at your center or school in light of the authors' statements about the complexity of counting. Do your methods provide insight as to the instructional needs of your students? If not, what change is needed?

Chapter 4: Number Operations
Every Operation Tells a Story

1. The authors caution against a focus on arithmetic and the symbols used to write equations in the early years. Do you agree or disagree? Why?

2. The Math Snapshots in this chapter describe several different ways that Ms. Green helps children model a problem situation. Which of these strategies do you see yourself using?

3. Select a child who is at the *direct-modeling* stage of problem solving. Ask the child to solve simple situations involving change or comparison. Watch how he or she models the story, noting use of manipulatives, fingers, or marks on a paper. Next, work with a child who uses *counting* strategies to solve the same problems. Compare your observations.

4. What factors affect the level of difficulty in a problem situation? How can you use these factors to adapt activities for the different developmental needs of children in your classroom?

5. The authors state that "every operation tells a story." What stories or books have you found to be successful in helping children make meaning of number operations? Is there a title from the recommended list you would like to try?

Chapter 5: Pattern
Recognizing Repetition and Regularity

1. It has been said that "mathematics is the science of patterns." After reading this chapter, do you agree? What makes patterns part of all mathematics?

2. What is a *unit of repeat*? How is it central to the Big Ideas of Pattern?

3. The Common Core State Standards (CCSS) for Mathematical Practice require students K–12 to "look for and make use of structure." How does early work with repeating patterns lay a foundation for this type of thinking?

4. The Math Snapshots in this chapter describe how Ms. Rosa recognizes children's natural interest in patterns and plans intentional activities to push their understanding further. Describe a time you observed children exploring patterns in their play. How did you respond? Would your response be different now, after reading this chapter? If yes, how so?

5. Look at the chart of activities for exploring patterns (Table 5.1). What kinds of activities do you see yourself using? Why?

Chapter 6: Measurement
Making Fair Comparisons

1. The authors suggest that traditional instruction in measurement moves too fast. What kind of foundational experiences do young children need *before* standard measurement?

2. In your mind, what makes a measurement "fair"? Compare your understanding to the understanding of a typical preschooler.

3. Ms. Marty, the teacher in this chapter's Math Snapshots, is described as an "intentional" teacher. What does this term mean to you? What percentage of your own math teaching would you say is *intentional*?

4. Consider the questions that build understanding about measurement (see Table 6.1). When are you most likely to hear children asking questions like these? Give an example of how you could *mathematize* one of those situations.

5. Describe the use of conventional measuring tools (rulers, measuring tapes, measuring cups, and so on) in your classroom by children and adults. Does this chapter change the way you think about the importance and role of conventional tools? If so, how?

Chapter 7: Data Analysis
Asking Questions and Finding Answers

1. In what ways does the Lost and Found investigation described in the Math Snapshots address the Big Ideas of Data Analysis?

2. An authentic problem—one whose solution is not obvious or predetermined—is a compelling reason to gather data. Give an example from your own classroom of a problem or question that motivated children to investigate data.

3. Look at the chart of types of data displays (Table 7.1). What kinds of graphs do you currently use? What other ones do you see yourself using? Why?

4. Describe any of your daily routines that include gathering data, such as attendance or recording the weather. To what extent do they help focus children on the Big Ideas of Data Analysis? What modifications might you consider?

5. The authors recommend spending a greater proportion of time analyzing the data results than collecting and organizing it. Do you agree? Why or why not?

Chapter 8: Spatial Relationships
Mapping the World Around Us

1. Children learn to move through space and handle objects from a very early age. As a teacher, how do you *mathematize* those daily experiences for children?

2. What are the linguistic challenges of describing relationships between objects and locations? Think in terms of your children; what percentage need language support? What are some of the strategies you use?

3. Research has documented gender differences in spatial ability, even before the time children enter kindergarten. Have you found this to be true in your classroom? If so, what do you do to address issues of gender equity?

4. Look at the chart of activities that build understanding of spatial relationships (Table 8.1). What kinds of activities do you currently use? What other ones do you see yourself using? Why?

5. What kinds of mathematical thinking are supported by block play? What might you say to an administrator or parent who questions the value of time spent playing in the block corner?

Chapter 9: Shape
Developing Definitions

1. Most kindergarten-readiness tests include naming common two-dimensional shapes. After reading this chapter, do you agree that this is an important skill to emphasize? Why or why not?

2. For children who don't attend to the attributes of a shape, but see the shape as a whole, have you developed activities to help them acquire this skill? What has been most effective?

3. Look at the shapes definitions again in Table 9.2 on pages 163–166. What questions do you still have?

4. What is your favorite shape book? Evaluate the illustrations in light of the authors's recommendation to provide children with diverse shape examples.

5. The Math Snapshots in this chapter describe how Mr. Barry develops a "Math Challenge" to build towers, which extends for a week. In your opinion, what is the value of continuing an activity over more than one day? To what extent are you able to do this in your own teaching?

Conclusion

1. Which of the Big Ideas has caused you to wonder the most? In what ways has your thinking about mathematics been changed by this book?

2. Mark any pages that you will want to return to later. What do you notice about the kinds of information you found helpful? What does that tell you about your own growth as a professional?

3. Identify which facets of your present math curriculum are most likely to help children construct an understanding of the Big Ideas.

4. Identify which facets of your present math curriculum are most likely to hinder or limit children's understanding of the Big Ideas.

5. What do you believe is the most critical change that needs to be made in order to improve the mathematics learning outcomes at your center or school? How might you begin to make that change?

Bibliography

Andrews, A., & Trafton, P. R. (2002). *Little kids—Powerful problem solvers: Math stories from a kindergarten classroom*. Portsmouth, NH: Heinemann.

Ball, D. L. (1988). *Knowledge and reasoning in mathematical pedagogy: Examining what prospective teachers bring to teacher education*. Unpublished doctoral dissertation, Michigan State University, Lansing.

Baroody, A. J., & Dowker, A. (2003). *The development of arithmetic concepts and skills: Constructing adaptive expertise*. Mahwah, NJ: Erlbaum.

Barratta-Lorton, M. (1977). *Mathematics their way*. Menlo Park, CA: Addison-Wesley.

Bowman, B. T., Donovan, M. S., & Burns, M. S. (Eds.). (2001). *Eager to learn: Educating our preschoolers*. Washington, DC: National Academy Press.

Carpenter, T. P., Fennema, E., Franke, M. L., Levi, L., & Empson, S. B. (1999). *Children's mathematics: Cognitively guided instruction*. Portsmouth, NH: Heinemann and Reston, VA: National Council of Teachers of Mathematics.

Chen, J. Q., & McCray, J. (2012). A conceptual framework for teacher professional development: The whole teacher approach. *NHSA Dialog: A Research-to-Practice Journal for the Early Intervention Field, 15*(1), 8–23.

Clements, D. H. & Sarama, J. (2009). *Learning and teaching early math: The learning trajectories approach*. New York, NY: Routledge.

Clements, D. H., Sarama, J., & DiBiase, A-M. (Eds.). (2004). *Engaging young children in mathematics: Standards for early childhood mathematics education*. Mahwah, NJ: Erlbaum.

Common Core State Standards. (2010). *Standards for mathematical practice*. Available at http://www.corestandards.org/the-standards/mathematics

Copley, J. V. (2010). *The young child and mathematics* (2nd ed.). Washington, DC: National Association for the Education of Young Children & National Council of Teachers of Mathematics.

Copple, C., & Bredekamp, S. (2010). *Developmentally appropriate practice in early childhood programs serving children from birth through age 8* (3rd ed.). Washington, DC: National Association for the Education of Young Children.

Copple, C. E. (2004). Mathematics curriculum in the early childhood context. In D. H. Clements, J. Sarama, & A-M. DiBiase (Eds.), *Engaging young children in mathematics: Standards for early childhood mathematics education* (pp. 83–87). Mahwah, NJ: Erlbaum.

Dehaene, S. (1997). *The number sense: How the mind creates mathematics*. New York, NY: Oxford University Press.

Duncan, G. J., Dowsett, C. J., Claessens, A., Magnuson, K., Huston, A.C., Klebanov, P., . . . Japel, C. (2007). School readiness and later achievement. *Developmental Psychology, 43*(6), 1428–1446.

Feiler, R. (2004). Early childhood mathematics instruction: Seeing the opportunities among the challenges. In D. Clements, J. Sarama, & A-M. DiBiase (Eds.), *Engaging young children in mathematics: Standards for early childhood mathematics education* (pp. 393–400). Mahwah, NJ: Erlbaum.

Fosnot, C. T., & Dolk, M. (2001). *Young mathematicians at work: Constructing number sense, addition and subtraction*. Portsmouth, NH: Heinemann.

Gentner, D., & Loewenstein, J. (2002). Relational language and relational thought. In E. Amsel & J. P. Byrnes (Eds.), *Language, literacy, and cognitive development: The development and consequences of symbolic communication* (pp. 87–120). Mahwah, NJ: Erlbaum.

Ginsburg, H. P., Kaplan, R. G., Cannon, J., Cordero, M. I., Eisenband, J. G., Galanter, J., & Morgenlander, M. (2006). Helping early childhood educators to teach mathematics. In M. Zaslow & I. Martinez-Beck (Eds.), *Critical issues in early childhood professional development* (pp.171–202). Baltimore, MD: Brookes.

Ginsburg, H. P., Lee, J. S., & Boyd, J. S. (2008). Mathematics education for young children: What it is and how to promote it. *Social Policy Report, 22*(1), 3–22.

Haylock, D., & Cockburn, A. D. (2008). *Understanding mathematics for young children: A guide of foundation stage and lower primary teachers*. Thousand Oaks, CA: Sage.

Hiebert, J. (1986). *Conceptual and procedural knowledge: The case of mathematics*. Hillsdale, NJ: Erlbaum.

Hill, H. C., Rowan, B., & Ball, D. L. (2005). Effects of teachers' mathematical knowledge for teaching on student achievement. *American Educational Research Journal, 42*(2), 371–401.

Hirsch, E. S. (1996 rev. ed.). *The block book.* Washington, DC: National Association for the Education of Young Children.

Hynes-Berry, M. (2012). *Don't leave the story in the book: Using literature to guide inquiry in early childhood classrooms.* New York, NY: Teachers College Press.

Kamii, C. (1982). *Number in preschool & kindergarten.* Washington, DC: National Association for the Education of Young Children.

Klein, A., & Starkey, P. (2004). Fostering preschool children's mathematical knowledge: Findings from the Berkeley Math Readiness Project. In D. H. Clements, J. Sarama, & A-M Dibiase (Eds.), *Engaging young children in mathematics: Standards for early childhood mathematics education* (pp. 343–360). Mahwah, NJ: Erlbaum.

Klibanoff, R., Levine, S. C., Huttenlocher, J., Vasilyeva, M., & Hedges, L. (2006). Preschool children's mathematical knowledge: The effect of teacher "math talk." *Developmental Psychology, 42*(1), 59–69.

Koralek, D. (Ed.). (2003). *Spotlight on young children and math.* Washington, DC: National Association for the Education of Young Children.

Ma, L. (1999). *Knowing and teaching elementary mathematics.* Mahwah, NJ: Erlbaum.

McCray, J. S., & Chen, J. Q. (2011). Foundational mathematics: A neglected opportunity. In B. Atweh, M. Graven, W. Secada, & P. Valero (Eds.), *Mapping equity and quality in mathematics education* (pp. 253–268). New York, NY: Springer.

McCray, J. S., & Chen, J. Q. (2012). Pedagogical content knowledge for preschool mathematics: Construct validity of a new teacher interview. *Journal of Research in Childhood Education, 26*(3), 291–307.

Moomaw, S. (2011). *Teaching mathematics in early childhood.* Baltimore, MD: Brookes.

National Association for the Education of Young Children. (2005). Early childhood mathematics: Promoting good beginnings. *A joint position statement of the National Association for the Education of Young Children (NAEYC) and the National Council for Teachers of Mathematics (NCTM).* Retrieved from http://www.naeyc.org/about/positions.asp

National Council of Teachers of Mathematics. (2006). *Curriculum focal points for prekindergarten through grade 8 mathematics: A quest for coherence.* Reston, VA: Author.

National Research Council. (1989). *Everybody counts: A report to the nation on the future of mathematics education.* Washington, DC: National Academy Press.

National Research Council. (2009). *Mathematics learning in early childhood: Paths toward excellence and equity.* Committee on Early Childhood Mathematics, Christopher T. Cross, Tamiesha A. Woods, and Heidi Schweingruber, Editors. Center for Education, Division of Behavioral and Social Science and Education. Washington, DC: The National Academies Press.

Richardson, K. (2012). *How children learn number concepts: A guide to the critical learning phases.* Bellingham, WA: Math Perspectives Teacher Development Center.

Schoenfeld, A. H. (1992). Learning to think mathematically: Problem solving, metacognition, and sense making in mathematics. In D. A. Grouws (Ed.), *Handbook of research on mathematics teaching and learning.* New York, NY: Macmillan.

Siegler, R. S., & Booth, J. L. (2004). Development of numerical estimation in young children. *Child Development, 75*(2), 428–444.

Sinclair, H., & Sinclair, A. (1986). Children's mastery of written numerals and the construction of basic number concepts. In J. Hiebert (Ed.), *Conceptual and procedural knowledge: The case of mathematics* (pp. 59–74). Hillsdale, NJ: Erlbaum.

Smith, S. S. (2013). *Early childhood mathematics* (5th ed.). Upper Saddle River, NJ: Pearson.

Sophian, C. (1999). Children's ways of knowing. In J. V. Copley (Ed.), *Mathematics in the early years* (pp. 11–20). Reston, VA: National Council of Teachers of Mathematics.

Van de Walle, J. A., & Lovin, L. *Teaching student centered mathematics, Grades K–3.* New York, NY: Allyn & Bacon.

Wiese, H. (2003). *Numbers, language, and the human mind.* Cambridge, UK: Cambridge University Press.

Index